SEEKING COMMON GROUND

SEEKING
COMMON
GROUND

PUBLIC SCHOOLS IN A DIVERSE SOCIETY

DAVID TYACK

HARVARD UNIVERSITY PRESS

CAMBRIDGE, MASSACHUSETTS

LONDON, ENGLAND

First Harvard University Press paperback edition, 2007

Library of Congress Cataloging-in-Publication Data

Tyack, David B.
Seeking common ground : public schools in a
diverse society / David Tyack.
    p. cm.
Includes bibliographical references and index.
ISBN-13 978-0-674-01198-4 (cloth: alk. paper)
ISBN-10 0-674-01198-8 (cloth: alk. paper)
ISBN-13 978-0-674-02420-5 (pbk.)
ISBN-10 0-674-02420-6 (pbk.)
1. Public schools—Social aspects—United States.
2. Education and state—United States.
3. Multiculturalism—United States.   I. Title.

LC191.4.T93 2003
379.73—dc21   2003049921

Designed by Gwen Nefsky Frankfeldt

#15.39

For Elisabeth, best of mates

Contents

SEEKING COMMON GROUND

Windows on the Past

WITHOUT losing a beat, policy talk about education has shifted back and forth in recent years between alarmist rhetoric and faddish solutions. The marketplace of ideas about schools brims over with sure solutions to persistent problems. I suggest a different stance because I do not believe that there are sure answers to the most important controversies in public education. These issues ebb and flow, and need to be renegotiated generation by generation. If one takes a long view of the development of public schools in a diverse society, certain basic motifs and puzzles recur. This book is about some of those recurrent and interactive themes of unity, diversity, and democracy.

In the ecology of democratic institutions, public schools have had a critical part to play. "The free common school system," Adlai Stevenson once said, "is the most American thing about America." The founders of the nation were convinced that the republic could survive only if its citizens were properly educated. This was a collective purpose, not simply an individual benefit or payoff to an interest group. Public school crusaders like Horace Mann believed that schooling should be a common good, open to all, benefiting all, as do clean water and air and leafy parks. The common school was to be public in control and funding. Above all, it was a place for both young and adult citizens to discover common civic ground, and, when they did not agree, to seek principled compromise. For much of our history locally controlled school districts were almost a fourth branch of government, a place where citizens could influence the future of the republic by shaping the education of the next generation.

Sometimes it didn't work that way at all. Often Americans did not check their political and religious differences at the schoolhouse door. Immigrants often resisted "Americanization." Open conflict arose in school politics between ethnic, religious, racial, and class groups. Despite the quest for consensus, it is hardly surprising in retrospect that prime civic institutions like schools were also sites of conflict. Nowhere was the gap between educational ideal and actual practice more apparent and painful than in the case of people of color. In periods of rapid political change and competing social values, public school politics and practices underwent major changes. Tensions have been inevitable.

A striking example of one such time of political contest and social transformation was the last half of the twentieth century. When I was starting as a teacher in the 1950s, a favorite liberal stance of educators toward social differences was to deny or ignore them. Professional educators were encouraged to be color blind and class blind and gender blind. Every American, after all, was an individual, and everybody was equal. If all people were not actually born equal, educators might at least act as if they were. Good schooling should mold good citizens according to a similar moral and civic pattern. Scholars tried to define a unique American Character and searched for the supposed political and economic consensus that unified the nation.

The Cold War rhetoric of national consensus masked gross social discrimination. In 1950 laws required racial segregation in the South, and bias against blacks was pervasive in the North as well. Hardly anyone noticed the flagrantly unequal educational and career opportunities open to girls and women. Textbooks in American history and literature paid scant attention to people who were not Anglo and not male (hence they ignored most citizens). General federal aid to public schools was a only a dim hope. Prayer and Bible reading were common practices in public classrooms, sometimes required by law. Most immigrants still came from Europe, not from Latin America and Asia.

Over the next few years, however, the more blatant forms of racial and sexual discrimination became illegal (though hardly extinct), federal aid mushroomed, textbooks became more culturally representative, the U.S. Supreme Court declared Bible reading and prayers unconstitutional, and most new immigrants were people of color. Activists formed social movements that challenged not only entrenched power and privilege but also entrenched beliefs. Criticizing traditional concepts of race, gender, ethnicity, and class, they sought to make schools more pluralistic in spirit and more egalitarian in practice. It did not take long for a conservative counter-reformation to appear in the Reagan years, as activists denounced many of the liberal reforms and "government schools" in general. They called for vouchers and school prayer. And so it went, educational advocacy without end.

This is a small book about a big topic. It explores how Americans attempted to create civic cohesion through education in a socially diverse and contentious democracy. I offer a few windows on the past and reflections on policy for people curious about how we have arrived at the present moment in our public school system. I have tried to attend to broad social forces but also to keep an eye on the daily lives of individuals, obscure and famous.

In the first part of the book I ponder some puzzles about the search for unity in public schooling. I ask why Americans, famous at home and abroad for distrusting government, chose to entrust the civic education of their children to public schools. And why did citizens who competed with each other in political parties for votes, in churches for members and souls, and in commerce for profits expect schools to be free of strife? Some of the founding fathers spoke approvingly of the "homogeneous" citizen as the ideal product of public schooling. They believed that Americans would remain free only to the degree that citizens shared political principles and civic virtues. Writers of history textbooks, for instance, wanted to instill patriotic literacy by teaching a master narrative, but even that proved controversial, for from the start citizens quarreled about who should be included and whose values should prevail.

In the second part I examine some of the ways educators have dealt with social diversity. I compare school policies that dealt with race, ethnicity, and gender, treating the categories as social constructions rather than as essential differences. Underlying the debates over these policies was a fundamental question: Are students basically the same or different? Race raised especially thorny issues. Scientifically, the concept of black and white "races" was nonsense, yet a policy of color blindness ran the danger of ignoring the powerful effects of institutional racism. The U.S. Constitution has given some policy guidance on race and religion, but there has been no separation of ethnicity and state. The treatment of European ethnic groups ranged from the hard-edged assimilation pushed by "Americanizers" to a culturally respectful stance. Usually the favored goal of educators was to produce an assimilated American individual, not to preserve cultural diversity. After World War I, however, more and more critics came to believe that the totally assimilated citizen was a fiction concocted by the loyalty police.

"Leave No Child Behind" is a modern motto, but the problem of academic failure is ancient. In American public schools educators have struggled from the beginning with the plight of students who failed academically. For classroom teachers this was one of the most important forms of diversity. Educators had many diagnoses and prescriptions for such pupils and disagreed about how to reach the children left behind. Were students mostly the same or mostly different? Should the "laggards" be tracked and given a separate curriculum, or should all students be helped to learn the same subjects?

In the third part of the book I look at democracy in educational governance. Serving on local school boards gave ordinary citizens a way to practice democracy, as Thomas Jefferson observed. A defining, and unusual, feature of public education in the United States has been its highly decentralized system of control by locally elected school boards. Despite the popularity of "democratic localism," professional educators and their elite lay allies did their best to "take the schools out of politics" by weakening local rule and eliminating school districts. They developed an alternative notion of "democracy" as government by experts, and they produced elaborate bureaucracies based on models of business efficiency rather than democratic theory.

In recent years there has been another challenge to local representative government in public education, this time coming from advocates of parental choice of schools and of financing by publicly supported vouchers. These reformers say there is too much democracy; it throws sand in the gears of education. The way to improve education is to turn schools into an enormous marketplace of private and public schools, to give parents vouchers for their children's education, and to solve the problems of governance and quality by letting the market do its work. Parents will choose wisely the schools that best serve their children.

Voucher-financed choice in a sense resolves the problems of democratic governance by dissolving them. No longer would people need to negotiate a sense of unified purposes or find ways to accommodate differences. Parents could choose, or help to create, schools that fit their values and goals. Left out of this plan, say critics, is the ability of citizens, whether parents or not, to make *collective* decisions about the education of the next generation through their elected school board representatives.

I invite readers to take a long view of how Americans in this diverse society have sought to use public education to build and preserve what the founders called a republic, and what we call a democracy. That task is ongoing today, and will never be easy or tension-free.

Why a long view, across time? History surely does not provide marching orders. It usually does not offer definite lessons. History can unsettle questions as well as settle them, for studying the past can help us to see that legacies we live with may not be so clear and entrenched as we thought. What history can do for citizens and educators who want to reflect on schooling is to provide a broader and deeper context for preserving what is good from the past, interpreting the present, and anticipating alternative futures. Whenever people try to understand their world, whether to change it or conserve it, they cannot avoid thinking in time. It is called memory, and without a sense of where we have been, it is easy to lose the way ahead.

PART ONE

UNITY

CHAPTER ONE

Schools for Citizens:
Preserving the Republic

Fᴿᴏᴍ the American Revolution onward, political and educational leaders have argued that the survival and stability of the republic depend on the wisdom and morality of its individual citizens. "I know of no safe depository of the ultimate powers of the society but the people themselves," Thomas Jefferson wrote in 1820, "and if we think them not enlightened enough to exercise their control with a wholesome discretion, the remedy is not to take it from them, but to inform their discretion by education." In 1822 New York Governor DeWitt Clinton declared that "the first duty of a state is to render its citizens virtuous by intellectual instruction and moral discipline, by enlightening their minds, purifying their hearts, and teaching them their rights and obligations." "It may be an easy thing to make a Republic," observed the educational reformer Horace Mann in 1848, "but it is a very laborious thing to make Republicans."[1]

Achieving civic unity by educating republican citizens was a daunting task. American society was socially diverse, scattered across a continent, politically contentious, religiously splintered, and averse to government. But the political and educational leaders who laid the foundations of civic education in the United States did believe that such unity was possible. Jefferson, Clinton, and Mann helped to persuade Americans that the educated character and trained mind of the individual was the safest foundation of public virtue, a better guarantor of proper civic beliefs and behavior than whole regiments of constables. An uneducated individual was an untrustworthy custodian of rights and liberties, but a properly schooled individual would recognize the bonds of obligation and principle that stabilize society and preserve freedom. Reformers spoke approvingly of free republicans as citizens who were "homogeneous" in their principles and behavior.[2]

A political philosophy of republican education resonated in the speeches of politicians and school leaders, in state constitutional debates, and in the history textbooks children read in school. In a nation roiled by partisan political battles, raw economic competition, and furious sectarian contests for church members and souls, educational leaders still thought it possible for citizens to agree on teaching a common denominator of political and moral truths. Political parties, ethnic groups, and religious sects, they thought, should suspend their conflicts at the schoolhouse door.[3]

Advocates of civic education often differed among themselves. Some feared anarchy and worried about protecting government from the people; others, more concerned about despotism, sought to protect the people from government. Horace Mann's religious foes claimed that his brand of moral teaching was just warmed-over Unitarianism, and Mann's political foes believed that his plan for civic education was just a bunch of Whig shibboleths. But the shapers of civic education did have enough in common to work together effectively and to create a set of founding principles and practices that lasted, with some changes, well into the twentieth century.[4]

The leaders of the common school movement at the state level shared similar social and economic backgrounds. They were white, male, prosperous, Protestant, and born in the United States. They expressed millennial religious hopes and political fears about the republican experiment. They wanted a religious, but nonsectarian, foundation for morality and sought to strengthen the character of individuals rather than appealing to the primordial claims of kinship and ethnicity. They tried to train the young to be politically non-partisan lest they be snared by frenzied political parties. And they believed that economic opportunity lay open to the virtuous and industrious school graduate.[5]

These common school crusaders were apt to assume that people like themselves were exemplars of worthy citizenship. Citizens who were native born, rural yeomen, Protestants, and not poor needed only to be reminded of their civic duties. Nativists saw the Irish as different, as people who had four strikes against themselves, since most of them were foreign born, poor, urban, and Catholic. As the people of the United States became more heterogeneous in religion, national origins, and cultures, educational leaders came to speak in more and more draconian tones about inculcating proper beliefs and behavior in students. Not surprisingly, when Irish Catholic leaders faced such raw ethnic and religious prejudice, they concluded that the public school was not for them. And all too often, people of color were not given a choice but excluded altogether from the "common" school.[6]

Racism, religious bias, ethnocentrism, and self-interest marred the search for a common denominator of civic instruction. But that is only part of the story. It is hard to find another reform in American history that spread as fast as the common school, had such an egalitarian rationale, and aroused so little dissent nationwide. In a society that offered few other government services, Americans created the most comprehensive system of public schooling in the world. During the nineteenth century at least, civic education was the public school's most crucial purpose.[7]

The nineteenth-century conception of civic education may seem distant and strange today, a time when critics deride "government schools" as bureaucratic, inefficient, and coercive, when some say that social pluralism precludes the possibility of a common civic education, when "culture wars" resonate in political conventions and in the academy, and when economic survivalism dominates the rhetoric of educational purpose. It is easier to deconstruct the ideas of the pioneers in civic education and their pedagogy of civic virtue than to reconstruct the world-view that made this civic education once seem plausible, indeed essential, to many citizens.

At certain times of tension, when the republic seemed threatened, Americans have become especially self-conscious about the civic values that the schools should teach. During periods of sharp demographic change, or war, or ethno-religious conflict, or economic challenge, for example, foundational principles of civic education came into sharper relief because they were less taken for granted. In this chapter I examine a few such episodes, focusing primarily on the ideas and actions of educational leaders.

In the half-century after the Revolution, for example, political and educational leaders worried about how to balance liberty and order. They sought to instill uniform republican values through schooling. The diversity that bothered them most was not ethnic or religious but political. They developed a durable set of principles of republican education even though it often took decades to actually establish the systems of public schools they advocated.

In the middle of the nineteenth century, when public education was spreading rapidly across the nation, common school crusaders searched for a political and religious common denominator for training future citizens. Sometimes contests over religion—particularly between newly arrived Catholics and nativist Protestants—tore communities apart. But citizens also settled a multitude of cultural issues amicably in their local school boards, as Benjamin Justice has shown. The urban contests over the reading of the Bible attracted a lot of attention but involved a relatively small proportion of the population. The pervasive fear of strong government and preference for local control meant that most disputes were settled locally.[8]

As the surge of "new" immigrants from southeastern Europe increased toward the close of the nineteenth century, educators became worried about how to assimilate the strangers into an Anglo version of the American political system. Elite reformers turned to the state to reshape civic education and to enforce their ideas of political and moral orthodoxy. They had two aims: to "take the schools out of politics" (meaning, usually, out of the hands of immigrant politicians); and to inculcate a nonpartisan and conformist version of citizenship, to take the politics out of students. "Americanization" became the war cry of anxious reformers.

The American faith in the power of civic education to change people became so compelling that the federal government itself used schooling as a follow-up to war and imperialism, a kind of pedagogical mop-up operation. Federal education of former foes began with attempts to "civilize" defeated native peoples. After the Spanish-American War federal officials created programs to "Americanize" colonial wards of the nation, such as Filipinos. After World War II, experts in civic education sought to "democratize" Japan.

Despite different circumstances in each case, the educational campaigns shared underlying ideologies. Efforts such as these were often more draconian than the Americanization programs aimed at immigrants, but they shared a common faith in the power of civic socialization to produce worthy citizens. The history of civic education in the United States presents unresolved tensions among competing values. Why did citizens who distrusted government decide to entrust the civic and moral training of their children to public schools? How did advocates of republican education reconcile individualism and homogeneity? Was it possible to have nonsectarian moral training and nonpartisan political instruction? How did educators treat the potential conflict between loyalty to state or nation and criticism of government?

Struggles over such questions resound in Americans' discourse about the political philosophy of education. They debated the value of political uniformity and diversity, individualism and group identity, liberty and order, and freedom from the state and freedom for the state to use its powers to socialize the young. Today there is lively debate about creating a curriculum that mirrors our cultural variety and equally vivid concern about teaching patriotism and common values.

But it would be a mistake to focus only on dissent. In the past, Americans have often agreed on the common moral values and political principles that should be taught to the young in public schools. And even today there may still be more agreement on the basic purposes of civic education than is commonly believed.

A Republican Charter for Education

The idea that the free republican was the uniform citizen becomes somewhat less puzzling if one recalls that balancing liberty and order in the new nation was an effort beset with danger and difficulty. Where along the spectrum from tyranny to anarchy would Americans find the proper synthesis of ordered liberty? A number of leaders in the early republic believed that republics had historically been as evanescent as fireflies on a summer evening, that monarchical Europe was conspiring to wreck the United States and to draw it into endless wars, that internal disorders and factions were threatening to shatter society, and that a continental nation composed of many states could not long remain republican.[9]

A deep foreboding about the future accompanied an equally deep millennial faith in the destiny of the new nation. In 1811 Thomas Jefferson wrote that "the eyes of the virtuous all over the earth are turned with anxiety on us, as the only depositories of the sacred fire of liberty, and . . . our falling into anarchy would decide forever the destinies of mankind, and seal the political heresy that man is incapable of self-government." What threatened this experiment, Jefferson thought, was political diversity more than ethnic or religious diversity—the population in 1790 was about four fifths of English descent, and it was overwhelmingly Protestant. Jefferson believed in literacy as a prerequisite for citizenship, but not in English only: a citizen, he wrote, must be able to "read readily *in some tongue,* native or acquired." What really bothered Jefferson was errors in political principles. A government based on false ideas was fatal to freedom and equality.[10]

Winning the war and building a new government was only the beginning, said Benjamin Rush, a signer of the Declaration of Independence, a physician, and an educational theorist. "We have changed our forms of government, but it remains yet to effect a revolution in our principles, opinions, and manners so as to accommodate them to the forms of government we have adopted. This is the most difficult part of the business of the patriots and legislators of our country." The schoolmaster and lexicographer Noah Webster agreed and proposed an "ASSOCIATION OF AMERICAN PATRIOTS for the purpose of forming a NATIONAL CHARACTER."[11]

From the beginning of the new nation, politicians and educators linked schooling to the preservation of the republic. The process of admitting new states into the Union illuminates one connection between schooling and republican values. From the start, Congress used the national domain to support common schools. The Ordinance of 1785 declared that "there shall be reserved the lot No. 16, of every township, for the maintenance of public schools, within the said township." In the Northwest Ordinance of 1787, which laid down the terms for creating new territories and states, Congress included this clause: "Religion, morality, and knowledge, being necessary to good government and the happiness of mankind, schools and the means of education shall forever be encouraged."[12]

Thus began a land-grant common school system of locally controlled schools, most of them one-room rural institutions. Over the nineteenth century Congress allotted three times more acreage to common schools than it did to the better known land-grant colleges. In ideology as well as finance, Congress helped to give the common school a continental reach.[13]

The U.S. Constitution required Congress to guarantee that new states had "a Republican form of Government." The founding fathers worried about the coherence and stability of a continental nation composed of different states carved from the vast public domain. What assurance could there be that the citizens of those states would share not only a commitment to republican liberties and duties but also an allegiance to the nation based on those principles? As time went by, both the Congress and territorial leaders who wrote constitutions for new states came to agree that public education was an essential feature of a republican government based on the will of the people.[14]

The founders believed it essential to expose the young to correct political ideas and to shield them from the wrong ones. Virtue should become a habit. Europe loomed as an ideological house of pestilence, a source of contagion. George Washington opposed educating Americans abroad, where they would run the danger of "contracting principles unfavorable to republican government." He believed that the "more homogeneous our citizens can be made" in principles, opinions, and manners, the "greater will be our prospect of permanent union." Political homogeneity was not a vice but a virtue. Jefferson agreed: "the consequences of foreign education are alarming to me as an American." Georgia went so far as to disbar its citizens from civic office for as many years as they studied abroad, if they went overseas when they were under the age of sixteen.[15]

The "homogeneous" American must study American textbooks, wrote Noah Webster: to use Old World texts "would be to stamp the wrinkles of decrepit age upon the bloom of youth and to plant the seeds of decay in a vigorous constitution." Webster's pedagogy of civic republicanism was moral as well as cognitive, religious as well as political in inspiration. The young, he thought, should learn the principles of representative and limited government and also should practice republican virtues. The prolific Webster, whose spellers had sold over twenty million copies by 1829, devised a "Federal Catechism" to teach these proper republican principles to children. He warned them of the evils of monarchy, aristocracy, and direct democracy, while praising the virtues of representative republics as embedded in the constitutions of the nation and the individual states. He also inserted a "Moral Catechism" that stressed virtues such as obedience, moderation, truthfulness, frugality, and industry.[16]

Textbook writers typically used statesmen like George Washington as exemplars of the republican character. As soon as the American child "opens his lips," said Webster, he "should lisp the praise of liberty, and . . . illustrious heroes." Rush agreed with Webster's policy of transforming American statesmen into demigods. Though he had not admired Washington's leadership during the war, he thought it prudent to tell less than the full truth about the founding fathers: "Let the world admire our patriots and heroes. Their *supposed* talents and virtues . . . will serve the cause of patriotism and of our country."[17]

Jefferson, of course, was a passionate apostle of religious and intellectual freedom. He gave to the University of Virginia a charter that proclaimed that the university "will be based on the illimitable freedom of the human mind." He also crusaded for "the diffusion of knowledge among the people" as an instrument of political progress. He advocated three years of public education for all white children in Virginia and proposed that only literate citizens be allowed to vote. But there were limits on the freedom he would endorse in civic education. Diffusion of what knowledge? There were too many erroneous and dangerous political principles in circulation to leave civic education to chance.[18]

Jefferson was especially concerned about the correct education of future leaders at the University of Virginia. He wanted to expurgate the Tory passages from the history book by the Scottish historian David Hume used at the university and to prescribe the textbooks used in government. "There is one branch [of knowledge]," he wrote to his fellow members of the Board of Visitors, "in which [political] heresies may be taught, of so interesting a character to our own state, and to the United States, as to make it a duty in us to lay down the principles which are to be taught. It is that of government." His aim was to make the University of Virginia a "seminary" of states rights principles and a foe of centralized government.[19]

Jefferson believed that children and youths could learn about citizenship from observing adults performing the duties of citizens in their local communities. He admired the direct democracy of the New England town meeting and proposed a similar "ward" system for Virginia. Local control of schools and other civic affairs not only was more efficient than centralized government but also was a bulwark of the people's liberties. "These little republics," said Jefferson of the wards, "would be the main strength of the main one" (the United States of America). What could hold together the intricate web of local, state, and national republics? A common set of principles and practices called republicanism.[20]

Benjamin Rush's concept of civic education sounded more draconian than Jefferson's. Rush argued that the best way to "render the mass of the people more homogeneous, and thereby fit them more easily for uniform and peaceable government," was to create schools that inculcated republican principles and attributes of character. "I consider it possible to convert men into republican machines. This must be done, if we expect them to perform their parts properly, in the great machinery of the government of the state."[21]

Rush, Webster, Jefferson, and a number of other educational theorists wanted to create schools that were public in finance and control, arranged into a system of lower and higher schools, and devoted above all to producing republican citizens. From the Revolution to Jefferson's death in 1826, most American schools remained heterogeneous rather than uniform and systematic, were private rather than public, and tended to perpetuate differences of social class, sect, and region rather than inculcating a universal republicanism. But the hope that a uniform public education could integrate the polity did not disappear. In the middle of the nineteenth century, during the common school crusade, the republican ideal vigorously returned, fortified by new anxieties and old claims.

The Common School and a Political Common Denominator

"The great experiment of Republicanism—of the capacity of man for self-government"—Horace Mann declaimed on the Fourth of July, 1842, "is to be tried anew." It had always failed before "through an inadequacy in the people to enjoy liberty without abusing it." As Mann, Secretary of the Massachusetts State Board of Education, looked about at Boston and the nation, he saw riotous mobs and selfish nabobs, votes bought or ignorantly cast, ill-educated citizens serving on juries and in the militia, impoverished children working in factories, and disputes over slavery sounding "firebells in the night."[22]

In Cincinnati at the same time, Mann's fellow common school reformer Calvin Stowe reminded his colleagues "that unless we educate our immigrants, they will be our ruin," for "to sustain an extended republic like our own, there must be a *national* feeling, a national assimilation." Immigrants can become "grafts which become branches of the parent stock . . . and not like the parasitical mistletoe." But in the period from 1830 to 1860, when the foreign-born increased faster, proportionately, than at any other time in American history, nativists took a much more hostile view of immigrants than Stowe did.[23]

After citing a litany of evils, educational crusaders like Mann turned to their Protestant-republican ideology for solutions. God had chosen America as a redeemer nation to prove that humans were capable of self-government. The educated character of the individual was the foundation of public virtue; the good society was an aggregation of such citizens. The common school, a public institution that mixed students from all walks of life, was to teach a common denominator of political and moral truths that was nonpartisan and nonsectarian. Political parties and religious denominations should stop their quarrels and competition at the schoolhouse door. Let civic education work its magic.[24]

All of this was easier said than done. Just how could state common school advocates and local school trustees find a religiously and politically neutral common denominator? Horace Mann thought he had the answer: Base moral teaching on the Bible, but make no sectarian gloss of Scripture. Did not everyone already believe in the basic individual virtues embedded in the Massachusetts constitution of 1780: industry, frugality, benevolence, charity, temperance, patriotism, justice, sobriety, and moderation? Who could object if the state tried to implant such traits in the young? Noah Webster's moral catechism stressed similar values, as did the California school reformer John Swett. In his 1885 book for teachers on "school ethics," Swett assumed that all citizens would agree with his textbook list of individual civic virtues: self-knowledge, self-restraint, temperance, honesty, obedience, punctuality, conscientiousness, impartiality, gratitude, friendliness, kindness, patience, frankness, seriousness, firmness, cleanliness, and courtesy. Similar moral traits were familiar and attractive, as I shall later suggest, in 1996 to the teachers and parents who answered a survey conducted that year on moral values in the classroom.[25]

Mann also proposed a consensual solution to the problem of political neutrality in civic education: Teach only republican principles that were universally approved "by all sensible and judicious men, all patriots, and all genuine republicans." If a teacher encounters a politically "controverted text," Mann advised, "he is either to read it without comment or remark; or, at most, he is only to say that the passage is the subject of disputation, and that the schoolroom is neither the tribunal to adjudicate, nor the forum to discuss it." Mann himself, though deeply opposed to slavery, rebuked the principal of a school for training teachers for taking students to an abolitionist meeting. That was far too controversial. It could bring ruin to the common school. But if students could share a moral and political common ground, he thought, they would later be less likely to fall prey to party passions and the politics of excess.[26]

The common school crusade and the teaching of American his-

tory moved in tandem. Before the Civil War six states required
public schools to teach American history, and between 1860 and
1900 another twenty-three mandated it, usually along with the
study of federal and state constitutions (included in most textbooks). The constitutions were regarded as sacred texts in many
parts of the country. In New Hampshire all pupils in the eighth
grade had to read the state and federal constitutions *aloud.*[27]

Textbook writers—driven by conscience, custom, and commerce—sought the same sort of consensual moral and civic instruction that Mann advocated, as I will show later. No textbook author
deployed the apparatus of consensus better than the Reverend
William Holmes McGuffey, whose school readers sold 60 million
copies during the period from 1870 to 1890 and a total of 122 million by 1922. The advertising blurb printed with his fourth reader
in 1844 assured the public that "NO SECTARIAN matter has been admitted into this work" and "NO SECTIONAL matter" (commenting on
slavery, for example) appeared.[28]

State education officers like Mann and Swett used their positions
as bully pulpits to proclaim the importance of nonpartisan civic education through the common school and to suggest school policies.
They had little power, however, to enforce laws or policy. Americans from the Revolution to the end of the nineteenth century became experts in hobbling the power of state governments. Citizens
distrusted legislators and state school officials. They abolished the
state school superintendency in Connecticut when Henry Barnard
held that position and nearly did the same thing to Horace Mann.
A German immigrant, fascinated by the dispersion of power in the
United States, wrote that "in America you can see how slightly a
people needs to be governed."[29]

School governance was not quite anarchy, though some of the
state school promoters thought it was. Local trustees made most of

the key decisions in most places, not courts, legislatures, or state officials, at least until late in the nineteenth century. Most moral and civic questions were settled by majority rule in most communities. This gave school boards some leeway to adapt to local circumstances—the religious and ethnic composition of the neighborhoods, for example—but local control could also be hard on minorities.[30]

Culture Wars

There were many Americans—notably, immigrant Irish Catholics—who did not share the world-view of the pietist school reformers or school trustees. Protestants and Catholics, newcomers and established groups, often talked past each other about issues like civic and moral education and on rare occasions engaged in mortal and sustained conflict that makes today's "culture wars" look like minuets. In 1844 in Philadelphia, for example, the Catholic bishop requested that Catholic children be allowed to use the Douai version of the Bible. Thinking that Catholics wanted to eject the Protestant Bible from the schools, a nativist mob attacked Irish Catholics and burned their houses and churches.[31]

Protestants and Catholics typically had quite different views of civic and moral education. As members of the Anglo-Protestant dominant group, the common school reformers usually did not recognize their own clannishness. They could not understand why their proposal of nonsectarian and nonpartisan schooling was not acceptable to all right-thinking people. By contrast, their Catholic opponents often regarded this "solution" as a devious ploy or a callous power play.[32]

A cartoon by Thomas Nast in 1871 captures the Anglo-Protestant nightmare of the destruction of true American institutions by Irish Catholics. The U.S. Public School stands in ruins while flags fly briskly over Tammany Hall. The teacher stands resolutely shielding his pupils, Holy Bible protruding from his coat, while alligators with bishop's mitres advance up the beach to devour the terrified children. Many Catholics despaired of finding any compromise on religion in the schools. Enrollments in Catholic parochial schools swelled. Catholics sought to have public funds channeled to the parochial schools they controlled—an issue that then and now has been vehemently contested. By 1890, about 626,00 students attended Catholic parochial schools, about 8 percent of the student population in public schools; by 1920 the ratio was 12 percent.[33]

Protestants and Roman Catholics each identified their different values with the common weal. A Kansas Protestant, reflecting the millennialism suffusing the common school movement, exclaimed that "Americanism is Protestantism . . . Protestantism is Life, is Light, is Civilization, is the spirit of the age. . . . Education with all its adjuncts, is Protestantism." To people like him, the common school was a symbol of patriotism, a means of rooting government in the virtue of free individuals.[34]

A Catholic leader expressed a more collective and traditional view that education should train the young to be "docile and respectful to their superiors, open and ingenuous, obedient and submissive to rightful authority, parental or conjugal, civil or ecclesiastical," and to obey "the precepts of the church." In such moral education, the young were to retain the loyalties of kin, sect, and ethnic group as well as learn a universalistic form of patriotism. Protestants stressed individual effort and character as the keys to success, but Catholics emphasized communal efforts.[35]

Ethnocultural disputes in the nineteenth-century public schools involved language and ethnicity as well as religion. They also arose when immigrants protested derogatory stereotypes in textbooks. Political issues that stemmed from differences of language and culture seemed less absolute and nonnegotiable than religious disputes. Though most school leaders preferred to use English as the language of instruction, some flexibility in linguistic policies seemed warranted. It was part of the common school mandate to attract all children to the public schools, including immigrants. In addition, local school boards wanted to win the support of prosperous ethnic groups, like the Germans, who had the money to create their own schools if they wished and the political clout to shape policies in common schools. In general, the Democrats were more favorably disposed than the Republicans toward cultural pluralism—whether the policies concerned alcohol or language. Democrats were delighted to see ethnocentric Republicans shoot themselves in the foot when they demanded in the 1880s and 1890s that English only be used in the classroom. There was strong voter backlash against such legislation in Massachusetts, Wisconsin, and Illinois.[36]

In some cities Germans pressed for bilingual schools; in others they simply sought the study of the language as a special subject. By 1900, 231,700 children were studying German in elementary grades. In Milwaukee, where working-class immigrants had gained political clout, children could attend classes in German, Italian, and Polish, while elsewhere they studied languages such as Norwegian, Czech, Spanish, and Dutch.[37]

In St. Louis in the 1870s Superintendent William T. Harris saw no conflict between eventual assimilation and the study of German, arguing that ethnic and family traditions "form what may be called the *substance* of the character of each individual, and they cannot be suddenly removed or changed without disastrously weakening the personality." He was arguing, in effect, that there was no reason that Germans should not be able to keep their culture while participating as citizens in American political institutions. That way, they would become assimilated more gradually but more firmly than if their culture had been ignored or suppressed. In Wisconsin, where state laws decreed teaching in English, a county superintendent said

in his annual report that it was better to look the other way when
he found that some public school classes were conducted in German. After all, he said, the Germans take great interest in education,
and if we alienate them they will abandon the public schools. Such
toleration for ethnic pluralism would change in the frenzy of World
War I. As a result of the anti-German laws and public opinion of that
time, the percent of youths in high school taking German dropped
from 24 in 1915 to less than 1 in 1922.[38]

To attract ever growing numbers of children to the common school,
leaders of public education during the nineteenth century had often
been willing to compromise on issues of cultural diversity. Political
control of education resided mostly at the local level, in the hands of
democratically elected school trustees. By and large, school leaders
thought that good schools and proper civic education could produce
good republicans. Environment counted. But by the turn of the century, more and more influential policy makers became willing, even
eager, to use the state to regulate education in new and sometimes coercive ways. New kinds of immigrants, from southeastern Europe,
seemed to need more than the traditional schooling. What kind of
civic training would it take, wondered Anglo policymakers, to make
these newcomers worthy of becoming Americans?[39]

Civic Education as Americanization

In 1909 a leader among the new generation of professional educators, Ellwood P. Cubberley, explained that southern and eastern
Europeans were of a different breed from their predecessors. The
solution was to break up their settlements and "to implant in their
children, insofar as can be done, the Anglo-Saxon conception of
righteousness, law and order, and popular government." His clause
"insofar as can be done" echoed the worries of the racialists of the

time that the "new" immigrants were genetically incapable of becoming true Americans. Complicating the task was the resistance to compulsory school attendance of some groups, such as Italians or Poles, who often distrusted state schools in the old country because they regarded them as imposed by an alien government.[40]

But Cubberley, like other educators who believed it possible to direct social evolution through schooling, was on the whole optimistic. He melded the certainty of a new "science" of education with the crusading moralism of predecessors like Mann. He believed that the school must take the place of older agents of socialization, "for each year the child is coming to belong more and more to the state and less and less to the parent." For the school to succeed in its new tasks, compulsory attendance and squads of truant officers were needed; the children of immigrants must be swept into the classroom.[41]

The elite reformers faced two tasks in coping with the civic education of immigrants, one political and the other educational. The political fox was in the pedagogical chicken coop. By the turn of the twentieth century, immigrants controlled much of urban education, sometimes through political machines and ethnic politics. How could such people produce citizens who measured up to the American standard? Cubberley believed it essential to take education out of politics, for in the cities the rabble all too often ruled. The state must strengthen the hand of the (Anglo-Saxon) experts who alone could refashion civic education so that it could accomplish the daunting task of Americanization. Then educators could train the young in democracy instead of being distracted by the riffraff bosses running the public schools of many large cities.[42]

In New York City over half the school staff members in 1908 were first- or second-generation immigrants. These veteran educators praised the decentralized ward system of the 1890s that "furnished an Irish Trustee to represent the Irishmen, a German Trustee to represent the Germans, and a Hebrew Trustee to represent the Hebrews." Wait, warned a senator during the debate on a charter to centralize control of the city's schools; this is the wrong model. We should put the children of the slums "under the influence of educated, refined, intelligent men and women, so that they will be elevated and lifted out of the swamp into which they were born and brought up." Only if the ethnic ward committees were abolished and the schools put under expert, nonpolitical control would the schools be able to accomplish the herculean task of turning southeastern European children into students who had the mentalities of Anglo-Saxons.[43]

The older informal kinds of political and social education had atrophied, reformers warned. Neither adults nor children gained the familiarity with the republican beliefs, rituals, and practices that had come from everyday discussions around the stove in the country store or from the rituals of party politics and Fourth of July oratory. The common school crusaders had assumed that a relatively brief exposure to the Three Rs and proper textbooks would round out the civic education the child gained in the family, in the church, from work on the farm or in the shop, and in the many other informal places to learn. But as Paula S. Fass has shown, in the Progressive era reformers believed that immigrant children who lacked the older patterns of socialization needed a hard-paced compensatory civic education.[44]

Learning English was essential (indeed, by the 1920s dozens of states had laws decreeing that instruction should be in English only). New York provided "steamer classes" for teaching English to immigrant youths just off the boat. Educators sped up the pace and amount of direct instruction in American history and government and required patriotic exercises like the Pledge of Allegiance (first used in New York in the 1890s), flag rituals, and elaborate celebrations of national holidays. They passed and enforced strong compulsory attendance laws. In this form of civic education, and in the new civic textbooks, good citizenship came to be more a matter of conforming to an Anglo, middle-class pattern of behavior than learning how the political system works or participating in politics. As in Horace Mann's day, educators shunned controversy.[45]

Sarah O'Brien's *English for Foreigners* (1909), aimed mostly at adults but sometimes used with children as well, had sections on the city, state, and national governments, citizenship, and the American flag (for that lesson students were to copy the sentence "America is another word for opportunity"). Under the lesson on citizenship the students learned that:

> The United States takes care of all its citizens and gives them many rights.
>
> A true citizen pays for his rights by obeying the laws, paying his taxes, and taking his part in protecting the government of the United States.
>
> The only way to make good laws is by choosing the right men to make the laws.[46]

This was a popular text for naturalization classes, partly because it gave approved answers for the civics test, but it also was a semi-official guidebook to the promised land for many immigrants.

Hannah Arendt claims that in the United States "education plays a different and, politically, incomparably more important role than in other countries." The reason, she says, is the diversity of America's population, the fact that it has been (and is) a land of immigrants in process of becoming citizens. But American citizenship has had a special, even universal, resonance apart from this fact, she believes, pointing to "the motto printed on every dollar bill: *Novus Ordo Seclorum,* The New Order of the World."[47]

Schooling as a Follow-up to War

The depth of the American faith in civic education becomes apparent when one looks at the repeated attempts to "Americanize" former enemies and colonial wards. A cartoon in *Judge* magazine in 1901 captured this belief in coercive transformation by education. Truant officer Uncle Sam is rounding up an American Indian, a Puerto Rican, a Filipino, a Cuban, and a Hawaiian while the teacher, Miss Columbia, stands outside the little red schoolhouse ringing her bell.[48]

When schooling became a follow-up to war, the ideology of civic education stood out in bold relief, and it is this ideology that I focus on here. The federal government had little control over mainstream public schools within the United States, but when it came to former foes, colonial subjects, or wards of the national state, military and federal officials had authority to define and enforce "Americanization." They did not conceive of this as inventing new goals or institutions; rather, they believed that they were expressing an American consensus. But in seeking to transform "the other," the former enemy or colonial ward, into an acceptable citizen, they became self-conscious about education's role in political and social transformation.

Three examples illustrate what I have in mind. The first is the attempt to solve the "Indian problem" by developing the Bureau of Indian Affairs (BIA) schools in the half-century after the Civil War. The second is the campaign to transform Filipino children into citizens in the years following the Spanish-American War. And the third is the move to "democratize" Japanese-Americans incarcerated in camps during World War II and to impose what Tochio Nishi calls "unconditional democracy" on Japan after the war.[49]

The three episodes of pacification by pedagogy had different origins and different outcomes, but there were some human links between them across generations. Soldiers who began their careers fighting and teaching Indians on the dry Great Plains ended up battling and instructing Filipino insurgents in the humid jungles of Luzon. Many of the administrators of the U.S. detention centers for Japanese-Americans had been educators in the BIA. A former teacher in the Philippines became head of education in the BIA during the Eisenhower years. Sometimes the role of soldier-teacher ran in families: Douglas MacArthur grew up on the Indian frontier where his father, Arthur, was an army officer; Arthur went from fighting Filipino guerrillas to setting up schools for them; and Douglas dictated the terms of democratic education in postwar Japan.[50]

People outside the federal government helped to define the character of education for "Americanization." A yearly conference of "Friends of the Indian" at Lake Mohonk near New Paltz, New York, for example, brought together white reformers with an interest in Indian affairs: members of associations devoted to Indian rights, soldiers, religious leaders, editors, university staff, members of the unpaid Federal Board of Indian Commissioners, and officials in the Indian Bureau. Through formulating and publicizing proposals and lobbying Congress and federal officials, this group had a large impact on Indian policy and helped to shape educational programs for Filipinos as well. Likewise, in the Philippines and in Japan commissions of nongovernmental lay experts and reformers—many of them academics—gained considerable influence over the policies adopted by the federal government. On occasion groups clashed, as when Catholics and Protestants fought over the kind of religious instruction Indian schools should provide and which textbooks should be used in the Philippines.[51]

Sometimes policy statements of federal officials and lay advisers betrayed doubt about the assimilability of the conquered. For the most part, however, they reveal faith in the power of education to transform the "savage" into a "civilized" citizen, the "little brown brother" into a modern man, and a once-hated Japanese foe into a good democrat. The participants at Mohonk, the members of the commissions, the army officers—these were typically Anglo-American native-born men, prosperous, well educated, Protestant, and with the self-confidence that comes from having one's opinion count.

In the early stages of Indian education, leaders were optimistic about how rapidly they could accomplish the aim stated by Richard Henry Pratt, the founder of the most famous boarding school for Indians, the Carlisle School: "Kill the Indian in him and save the man." Indians need not vanish, said the Commissioner of Indian Affairs in 1890, for they could be educated "to become absorbed into the national life, not as Indians, but as Americans." If enough "schools were established to give each youth the advantages of three to five years of schooling, said the Secretary of the Interior in 1883, "the next generation will hear nothing of [the Indian problem] and we may leave the Indian to care for himself." No need for troops or welfare doles. Armies can subdue Indians, but only educators can eradicate Indianness.[52]

Common themes emerge when these policymakers spoke about the relation of education to citizenship. They agreed about the importance of individualization, of divorcing the Indian from the tribe, the Filipino from the "feudal" system of the Spaniard, or the Japanese from the tyranny of emperor-worship. Before wards could become "free" they first had to become individuals taught to exercise their rights and liberties responsibly. Schooling was designed to break the hold of the group over the person and to link individuals to an idealized version of an open society and a republican political system.

These "individuals," however, had to become culturally alike in certain respects. The education of Indians illustrated the point. Reformers like Pratt spared no details in their campaign to transform outsiders into citizens. They attended to dress, athletics, vocational training, learning English, and traits like punctuality, industry, and discipline. Typically they saw such customs and values not as culturally specific but as universals held by "civilized" individuals. Pratt regarded his students as blank slates easily inscribed. They would soon forgo their past and embrace the latest stage of Euro-American civilization. A missionary to the Sioux described in 1901 the cavalier faith that schooling by itself would create uniform republican persons from many native peoples: "Uncle Sam is like a man setting a charge of powder. The school is the slow match. He lights it and goes off whistling, sure that in time it will blow up the old life, and of its shattered pieces he will make good citizens."[53]

In his instructions to BIA educators on "inculcation of patriotism in Indian schools," Commissioner Thomas Jefferson Morgan insisted that Indian students should acquire a new past on the way to a new future: "special attention should be paid . . . to the instruction of Indian youth in the . . . lives of the most notable and worthy historical characters. While in such study the wrongs of their ancestors cannot be ignored, the injustice which their race has suffered can be contrasted with the larger future open to them, and their duties and opportunities rather than their wrongs will most profitably engage their attention." In the process of "exciting . . . ambition after excellence in character" the teachers, he said, "should carefully avoid any unnecessary reference to the fact that they are Indians." He apparently forgot his own advice when he spoke to Indian students in a chorus at Hampton Institute: "As I sat here and listened with closed eyes to your singing, you were not Indians to me. You sing our songs, you speak our language. In the days that are coming there will be nothing save his color to distinguish the Indian from the white man."[54]

Although the eventual goal was to integrate the former foes or

wards into the larger society, well socialized, the federal government often segregated them: Indians in boarding schools or in day
schools on the reservation, Japanese-Americans in detention camps,
and Filipinos in garrison towns protected by the military from rebels
who did not want the children to become Americanized. It is not
coincidental that the Carlisle School originated as an educational
program for a group of intractable Indian warriors. Pacification by
pedagogy sought to destroy one identity and impose another, a
campaign notable for its illusory optimism and draconian arrogance. In some ways educating the enemy resembled the campaign
to "Americanize" the "new" immigrants from the old world.

Inevitable Tensions in Moral and Civic Education

"If there is any fixed star in our constitutional constellation, it is that
no official, high or petty, can prescribe what shall be orthodox in
politics, nationalism, religion, or other matters of opinion or force
citizens to confess by word or act their faith therein." So spoke the
U.S. Supreme Court in *Barnette* in 1943 in a case affirming the right
of schoolchildren to refuse to salute the American flag because
they were Jehovah's Witnesses.[55]

Only three years before, the Supreme Court had held that the
need for national unity transcended individual rights or diversity of
beliefs. Refusal to salute the flag, it said, was punishable insubordi-
nation. It was not for the Court to question "the wisdom of training children by those compulsions which necessarily pervade so
much of the educational process."[56]

These contrasting decisions highlight inevitable tensions in civic
education between liberty and unity. In a society so diverse, who
should prescribe what should be taught? And is unity a feasible—indeed, desirable—goal? How can freedom to dissent coexist with a
cohesive school and coherent society?

From Rush's call for schools to produce "republican machines" to the crusade to Americanize America during World War I to the Cold War years of the 1950s to the present, anxious advocates of civic education continued to believe that the American republic was an endangered experiment (although the threats changed from one time to another). Only if the common school could produce worthy citizens, they said, would the nation's future be assured. In a society rife with conflict and competition, all children had to be taught the values they should hold in common. Such a sense of common identity and destiny was not a luxury but a necessity in a republic; homogeneity of citizens was not a fault but a virtue.

At least on the surface, consensus on what moral values to teach young citizens was not hard to achieve. As Mann and Swett suggested, it was easy enough to find agreement on values such as honesty, kindness, and industry. During the nineteenth century, many states passed laws enjoining teachers to foster such virtues. In 1878 the Minnesota legislature, for example, passed an "Act to introduce Moral and Social Science in the Public Schools of the State." All school officers were expected to teach the same thirty-one moral traits—for example, self-respect, perseverance, and pity—at the rate of one a day (the day following the teacher's presentation on the virtue, pupils were to give examples of the practice of the virtue). Educators wanted moral education of this sort to permeate the curriculum, not simply to be taught in a particular course (though American history textbooks, analyzed in Chapter 2, were the ark of the patriotic covenant). Teachers at all levels were expected to exemplify the republican virtues.[57]

Although American society has become strikingly diverse, these Minnesota virtues have not disappeared. Consensual civic values are still alive and well in many schools and communities. A survey in 1996 of public school teachers reveals the resilience of traditional civic values and the resistance to controversy in the schools. A majority believed that teaching common core moral values was more important than teaching academics. Noah Webster and John Swett would not have been surprised that 95 percent of teachers thought honesty an essential lesson to teach; 90 percent, punctuality and responsibility; and 83 percent, industriousness. Three quarters thought that schools should stress that "democracy is the best form of government." Three quarters thought that the public schools should "help new immigrants absorb language and culture as quickly as possible, even if their native language and culture are neglected." Relatively few teachers (6 to 13 percent) wanted to introduce into their classrooms divisive issues such as "arguing that racism is the main cause of the economic and social problems blacks face today," "bringing in a speaker who advocates black separatism," or "bringing in a guest speaker who argues that the Holocaust never happened."[58]

The search for consensus and avoidance of controversy in civic education has left a mixed legacy. Consider Horace Mann's aversion to teaching students about controversial questions. Too much conflict of values, he believed, would drive parents away from the public schools. And today, many teachers worry that introducing value-fraught issues could disrupt the tenuous order of their classrooms or lead to legal challenges in a litigation-prone society. Yet if the public school could teach only about those matters on which people supposedly agreed, how would students learn to understand or manage their fundamental differences either as youths or as adult citizens? Avoiding controversy has sometimes made the school a buttress of the status quo, a "museum of virtue" disconnected from everyday life.[59]

As Mann and countless educators since him have discovered, it has been impossible to put a lid on civic education: Free people did disagree, and they mobilized others to bring about change. In the last generation, policies in civic education have perhaps been more sharply contested than ever before in our history, as many groups previously excluded from the debate over the teaching of values have sought to align instruction in public schools with the pluralistic character of the American people, to redefine the meaning of "American" both in the past and the present. "In the end," says the historian Jonathan Zimmermann, "debating our differences may be the only thing that holds us together." Trying to find a creative balance in civic education between commitment to democratic processes, common values, and respect for differences continues to be an enduring tension in schools for citizens.[60]

CHAPTER TWO

Patriotic Literacy: History Textbooks

Ready for the test?

What country did we fight during the Revolutionary War?
Who said, "Give me liberty or give me death"?
Why did the Pilgrims come to America?
Which president is called the "father of our country"?
Who wrote the *Star-Spangled Banner?*
What is the Fourth of July?
Who wrote the Declaration of Independence?

No, THIS is not a quiz for fifth-graders who have just completed a unit on early America. It is a set of questions chosen from a list of "100 Typical Questions" put on the Internet in 1993 by the Immigration and Naturalization Service to help immigrants prepare for the civic exam they had to take to win U.S. citizenship.[1]

This test of civic literacy included four questions about George Washington, two about Abraham Lincoln, and one each about Benjamin Franklin, Francis Scott Key, Patrick Henry, Thomas Jefferson, and Martin Luther King, Jr. (the only figure from the twentieth century). Four questions dealt with the Pilgrims and Thanksgiving and thirteen were about the Constitution. My immigrant grandfather probably could have answered most of the questions correctly when he became a citizen in 1889.

Michael Frisch, a historian at the State University of New York at Buffalo, found that these patriotic icons were fresh in the memories of his students in the 1980s. He asked them to list ten names that they associated with American history through the Civil War. Up popped Washington, Jefferson, Franklin, and other political and military leaders. The only woman among the top twenty-four mentions was Betsy Ross.[2]

It seems that traditional history is alive and well in the minds of immigration officials and college students in Buffalo. It thrives also in the U.S. Senate. On January 18, 1995, Republican Senator Slade Gorton rose to complain that a new set of National History Standards slighted the virtues of the founding fathers. "According to this set of standards," he lamented, "our students will not be expected to know George Washington from the man in the Moon." "Paul Revere and his midnight ride will never capture the imagination of our children," he warned, and "Ben Franklin's discovery of electricity will not encourage young scientists to seek out their own discoveries that can change the world." After complicated parliamentary maneuvering, ninety-nine senators voted for a resolution to grant federal money for development of history standards only to people who have "a decent respect for the contributions of Western civilization, and United States history, ideas and institutions, to the increase of freedom and prosperity around the world."[3]

To students and to many of their teachers school history has been synonymous with "real history." Frances Fitzgerald, the author of *America Revised*, recalled that she and her fellow students "believed in the permanence of our American-history textbooks . . . those texts were the truth of things: they were American history . . .

[they] had the demeanor and trappings of authority. They were weighty volumes. They spoke in measured cadences: imperturbable, humorless, and as distant as Chinese emperors." History textbooks have been a major means of civic education in the U.S. They reveal what adults thought children should learn about the past and are probably the best index of what teachers tried to teach young Americans. History texts have given the past a patriotic gloss, varnishing familiar icons and perpetuating familiar interpretations.[4]

Even though history textbooks have been, by most accounts, very dull, they have also been highly controversial. People have wanted history texts to tell the official truth about the past. The search for a lowest civic common denominator has often resulted in terminal blandness, but even then, critics have argued that the history texts did not get the public truth right. Textbooks resemble stone monuments. Designed to commemorate and *re-present* emblematic figures, events and ideas—and thus to create common civic bonds—they have also aroused vigorous dissent.[5]

As Jonathan Zimmerman has shown, many groups—not just middle-class Anglo Protestants—insisted that their own truths should prevail. In a nation so diverse socially and economically, and with such a mix of politically active associations, it would have been surprising if there had not been conflict over the official truths of the textbooks. Irish-Americans, for example, complained in the 1850s that histories were anti-Catholic and in the 1920s that they were too Anglophile. Southerners protested Yankee bias and vice versa. The National Association for the Advancement of Colored People (NAACP), beginning early in the twentieth century, demonstrated that blacks were either ignored or stereotyped in textbooks. Conflicts often intensified in times of tension when loyalty police went on alert and social activists recruited allies. The present history wars are a late chapter in a long book.[6]

In recent decades history textbooks, new and old, have come under attack for focusing too narrowly on what white, male, Anglo politicians and generals did. Textbook writers, said critics, neglected other groups—such as women and Hispanics—and their needs and achievements. Traditional history ignored everyday life and disrespected diversity. Only white, Protestant, Anglo men appeared as the doers of history; the rest were outsiders whose opinions and values and experiences counted for little.[7]

It is now easy to see much that is wrong with this "school history." It is less easy, perhaps, to understand how this traditional version came about and lasted so long, what its purpose and message were, why texts so resembled each other, and what issues proved to be controversial in different times.

Civic Purpose and Message

After the Revolution, there was one overwhelming motive for teaching history to schoolchildren and youths: creating good citizens. Over and over again, the prefaces of textbooks in history spoke of good citizenship. In 1852 Emma Willard reminded teachers and parents that "there are those who rashly speak, as if in despair of our republic, because, say they, political virtue has declined. If so, then is there the more need to infuse patriotism into the breasts of the coming generation."[8]

The compilers defined what they took to be civic literacy. To sell their books they appealed both to national pride and to personal fear of patriotic illiteracy. Well-taught students would be "so familiar with the lives and sayings of famous Americans that they will

have no difficulty in understanding" references to them in newspa-
pers said a best-selling textbook writer, Charles A. Goodrich, in
1867. Once established as textbook heroes, historical figures became part of the canon, people of whom "no one would be willing
to confess himself ignorant."[9]

Textbooks writers wanted youths to "love, honor, and emulate"
a common group of heroes—Columbus and Pocahontas, Patrick
Henry and Francis Scott Key, Robert Fulton and Benjamin Franklin,
Daniel Webster and Daniel Boone, Abraham Lincoln and George
Washington, among others. Goodrich, whose histories had sold
about half a million copies by 1870, wrote that "history sets before
us striking instances of virtue, enterprise, courage, generosity, patriotism, and by a natural process of emulation, incites us to copy
such noble examples. History also presents us with pictures of the
vicious ultimately overtaken by misery and shame, and thus solemnly
warns us against vice."[10]

Textbooks generally portrayed heroes as above party or sect. Educators mostly agreed that the civic and moral education of the
young should be nonpartisan and nonsectarian—so, too, the books
used in the common school. In the 1850s the reformer and textbook writer Elizabeth Peabody warned that whether America fol-
lows the bad example of the Old World or the promise of the New
"depends on young Americans, who are now sitting in classrooms
all over the country." They must learn civic truths "while they are as
yet unsolicited by party interests." In the years from President Jackson to President McKinley—a time of fierce political contests and
relentless party loyalty—few adults would have thought it possible
to have democracy without some form of "party interests." But it
was just such a nonpartisan message that textbooks taught schoolchildren.[11]

In the nineteenth century the pioneer compilers of "school histories" mostly treated the same topics. The overarching theme was the Providential progress of the "land of the Pilgrim's pride," and the Pilgrims became the template for worthy Americans. The narrative in this real history started with the "discovery" of the New World and colonization, told the triumphant story of Independence and the Revolution, and celebrated the creation of the Constitution. The history textbooks then organized their story around the administrations of President after President.[12]

Throughout the nineteenth century and well into the twentieth, this basic story proved durable, even during periods of social and economic transformation. After new groups of immigrants appeared from distant shores, the texts still remained Anglo-centric. When massive cities and industries transformed everyday lives, the authors continued to celebrate old-fashioned rural life and its virtues. When groups criticized this template of real history, they rarely attacked its theme of progress or the icons the texts celebrated. Instead, the protesters generally wanted to add their own heroes to the hall of historical icons. They wanted to be included in this saga of nation-building.[13]

Not surprisingly, given the fact that textbooks dealt chiefly with exploration, battles, and statesmanship, the most celebrated virtues were courage, persistence, endurance, and daring—qualities captured in the picture of Washington crossing the Delaware that faithfully adorned text after text. These traits were typically gendered as male. But history texts and school readers such as the ubiquitous McGuffeys could also teach other, more universal, virtues of the sort symbolized by pictures of the Pilgrims and their Thanksgiving. As mentioned in Chapter 1, states such as Minnesota frequently mandated the virtues that teachers were to instill in the young of both sexes. They also legislated that textbooks must be nonsectarian and nonpartisan. In most schools the textbook provided the entire history curriculum, and this gave extra weight to its pronouncements.

Textbooks Beget Textbooks

One reason nineteenth-century history textbooks resembled each other in their format and messages is that their compilers shared similar ideologies and social backgrounds. Before the Civil War, most of these authors were ministers, teachers, and writers living in the Northeast, especially in New England. They tended to be conservative Protestants, notables in their local communities. Most of them shared a similar Protestant-republican ideology that invested the American experiment with cosmic significance. America was, literally, God's country, the place He had chosen for the regeneration of mankind.[14]

Most of the early textbook authors did not claim originality. When they called themselves compilers, they meant that they were giving students access to everyday truths, ideas that were basic and noncontroversial, not original. Millennial views similar to those in textbooks were staples of sermons in churches and Fourth of July speeches. After the Civil War professional historians and career educators wrote a number of the texts. Explicitly religious lessons diminished in the texts, but the use of heroes as moral and civic models continued to flourish. So did the idea that all youths should achieve patriotic literacy.[15]

Another pressure toward uniformity in school history texts came from state laws that mandated the teaching of the subject. The major market for the texts was the upper grades of public elementary schools (very few students went on to high school in the nineteenth century). Common schools had explicit civic purposes. Recognizing this, states passed laws specifying what sort of history texts to use (nonsectarian, nonpartisan, and of a certain quality and price range, for example).[16]

The common school crusaders and textbook writers shared similar views of civic education. In the nineteenth century twenty-nine states required public schools to teach American history, often specifying special attention to the U.S. and state constitutions. By ear and eye, and if need be, by hickory stick, all children were to learn the sacred documents of the nation. As schools became more bureaucratized and similar in curriculum, texts became more standardized. In the second half of the nineteenth century school superintendents and principals wrote texts specifically designed for particular grade levels in urban systems.[17]

Commercial forces also fostered conformity in textbooks. Publishing American history texts was a rapidly expanding business, but a tricky one fiscally. Publishers wanted to make profits and avoid risks. Early in the century the format and themes of texts varied somewhat, but when certain history books sold well, they became the compilations to copy. Through imitation, textbooks became much alike in heroes, topics, judgments, and central message. Textbooks begat textbooks. They still do.[18]

The proliferation of laws requiring the study of history and the explosive growth of public schools in the nineteenth century created a strong market demand for textbooks, met first by compilers and printers producing for local or regional markets, and eventually prompting the growth of large textbook conglomerates selling millions of volumes.

In the 1890s several of the largest companies joined forces to become the American Book Company. It became known as "the book trust" and controlled about 80 percent of the textbook market. Contradicting the pieties of the textbooks they sold, some of the companies retailing American history texts engaged in cutthroat sales tactics. Salesmen bribed and blackmailed school boards and educators, mastered the craft of legislative politics, and offered deep discounts only to raise prices when their competitors wilted. There was a Jekyll and Hyde quality to the textbook business, as salesmen red in tooth and claw hawked primers on patriotic virtue. The histories used in public schools portrayed dead statesmen as civic paragons while living robber barons and politicians of the latter nineteenth century practiced corruption on a monumental scale.[19]

The Pedagogy of Patriotism

Most American history textbooks were "inexpressibly dull," said Edward Channing, a man who had reason to know, for he was a textbook writer as well as a Harvard professor of history. It is ironic that Channing found textbooks so boring, for nineteenth-century Americans regarded history as a major branch of literature and lionized superb story-tellers like Francis Parkman and George Bancroft, who wrote about exploration, battles, and the rise of democracy. Reading Parkman or William Hickling Prescott aloud around the fireplace was a favorite recreation of the middle and upper classes. This history for literate adults was similar to school histories in the topics it treated, but in style and tone the textbooks were another genre.

A few authors of textbooks—skilled writers such as Thomas Wentworth Higginson and Edward Eggleston—believed that children should be drawn to history, and to virtue, by engaging stories about admirable people. But few textbook writers believed that "school histories" should be entertaining. Indeed, they rendered dull books even worse by the pedagogy that they recommended.[20]

Much of the dullness of school history resulted from a wooden pedagogy that stressed memorizing desiccated facts. Many of the books were typographical horrors, with bold-faced subtitles and dark and light print of various sizes. The author of one best-selling history explained that the "portion of the work which is in large type embraces the leading subjects of history, and should be committed to memory by the pupil. That part which is in smaller type should be carefully perused." The organization of most history texts into numbered paragraphs assisted the teacher in conducting recitations, but critics argued that numbers and subheads amputated interest and turned history into disconnected facts rather than an absorbing narrative. As if to reassure students that the agony of reading history would soon be over, book titles announced that the texts were *short, condensed, abridged,* or *brief.* One author calculated that if students recited two pages a day of his "concise" text, they would be done in half a year.[21]

The tone of most textbooks was authoritative—they did not invite debate. The authorial voice sometimes sounded like God in the Old Testament, while the division of text into numbered paragraphs resembled the numbered chapters and verses of Scripture. Many textbooks had catechisms of set questions and answers similar to those in religious tracts. One minister from Massachusetts wrote this Yankee-centric catechism in geography:

Which is the highest mountain in the United States?
Mount Washington, one of the White Mountains in New Hampshire.[22]

The textbook was the source of knowledge, and the teacher's job was to make sure that the students acquired it. In the prefaces to their textbooks—resembling teachers' guides—compilers often discussed how to teach. Most educators appear to have used the recitation mode of teaching, in which students read a text and then recited what they learned as the teacher questioned and corrected the pupils. Authors did disagree, however, about whether pupils should recite the text word for word from memory or should put the lesson in their own words. The advocates of memorization argued that a good book should express ideas better than any child could do. Through memorizing the text students gained richer vocabulary and diction. If that was not the case, then the teacher should use another textbook. But others thought that students should present the assignment for the day in their own words, demonstrating to the teacher that they understood what it meant.[23]

Progress

The template of political and military topics varied little from textbook to textbook. The books typically began with the European "discovery" of North America, the planting of colonies by different nations and the military squabbles between them, independence from Britain and the Revolutionary War, the formation of the new government and the writing of the Constitution, foreign wars and foreign policy. Typically the texts included the Declaration of Independence and the Constitution as appendices.

After the Constitution came the administrations of the Presidents, one following another like brief dynasties—on the flyleaf of his history text one boy scribbled: "Memorize the dates and the sequence of the Presidents," indicating their importance as organizers of the story. Snippets of historical events and trends that didn't fit this military and political mold were typically mushed together into disconnected chapters under the cheerful name "Progress of Civilization."[24]

History textbooks, as a whole, had a strong master narrative in the nineteenth century: Its motif was that the United States was a favored nation. The ministers, teachers, and professional authors who wrote the prewar texts usually told an anxious tale of progress through the aid of Providence. In the textbooks of the second half of the nineteenth century the writers were often professional historians or school administrators, and they began to assign technology and the economy a more active role than God in the progress of the nation.[25]

The theme of progress was reassuring, but how could a favored nation be born in revolution and then torn by fratricidal war? How could textbook compilers frame those two events as Providential and progressive? It was easier to domesticate the Revolution than to explain the Civil War. By stressing the conservative virtues and opinions of the founding fathers the compilers of textbooks sought to tame the Revolution. It was over. One revolution was enough for any country. "Happy is that people whose God is the Lord," declared Charles A. Goodrich in the forty-fourth edition of his history in 1836. He left no doubt that America was God's country.[26]

The persistent conflict between North and South was far more ominous, far more difficult for textbook compilers to incorporate into their tale of progress than was the American Revolution. The war itself was less a problem than the politics and ethics of slavery. Writers were at home with military history and could treat the conflict as armed battles. But the ideology of the nonpartisan school and textbook gave little guidance in political conflicts as harshly polarized as the conflict over slavery.

A few Yankee authors condemned slavery and regarded the Civil War as a "purifying fire." Some applauded Reconstruction as an attempt to secure social justice and full citizenship for blacks. But mostly they tiptoed around the civic and moral issues involving race as if they were a minefield. Southerners, by contrast, repeatedly attacked what they regarded as the biases in northern textbooks, and during the war and its aftermath Confederate educators

produced their own compilations of real history. The South lost the
Civil War, but it was determined not to lose the textbook war.[27]

One way that northern textbook writers dealt with controversies
over race was to change the subject. A convenient distraction occurred in 1866, just as the war ended: the successful laying of the
Atlantic telegraph cable. Many authors of American history texts
gave cheerful accounts of this event right after describing the hor-
rific battles of the Civil War. The cable symbolized advance through
technology, comity through communication, a more peaceful path-
way to progress than the moral fervor of those who defended or attacked slavery. It was easier to be nonpartisan and nonsectarian
about laying the telegraph cable than about race or religion. But
even that achievement had sectional overtones: A Confederate
textbook claimed that the person who contributed the most to the
trans-Atlantic cable was not the northerner Cyrus Field, who got
most of the credit, but the Virginian Matthew F. Maury, a scientist
who was responsible for mapping the floor of the North Atlantic,
doubtless "the greatest contribution to man's geographical knowledge that has ever existed."[28]

Race, Religion, and Region

The textbook author William Swinton boasted that he had
achieved "a tone of treatment free from partisan bias of sectional-
ism, politics, or religion,—a tone of treatment as completely as possible *American*." The best stance was one of friendly neutrality
toward controversial views. It was also commercially smart not to
offend textbook customers and politically proper not to alienate
citizens from the common school, but such neutrality seemed
fraught with irony and contradiction. The textbook's heroes might
have seemed nonpartisan, but they hardly matched the reality of

the actual political party system, one that was quintessentially partisan. A rapacious textbook trust tried to monopolize the sale of histories of civic virtue. And when state legislatures banned "sectarian" and "partisan" textbooks, they typically meant books that told a story different from the conventional truths of the neighborhood and region and dominant ethnocultural group.[29]

The Three Rs of controversy over history textbooks—religion, race, and region—repeatedly threatened nineteenth-century efforts to base instruction on a moral and civic common denominator. But there never had been a golden age of consensus on textbooks. Before the Civil War, religious differences probably ignited most battles over bias in textbooks. Combatants often found their opponents incomprehensible as well as wicked. The religious liberal Horace Mann arm-wrestled with his orthodox ministerial critics about what books to include in school libraries, while Irish Catholics were incensed at "anti-papist" remarks in texts and at ethnic slurs presented as simple fact. Such controversies fueled the growth of Catholic parochial schools and the development of Catholic textbooks.[30]

In 1858 John Gilmary Shea wrote a "school history" designed to "supply a long felt want, especially in Catholic establishments" for a book that did not reflect the biases of New England Protestants. He was especially eager to give the Irish their due attention. "The Irish, who were great navigators and sea-rovers, discovered Iceland." In Shea's book the Spanish were not the unmitigated villains portrayed in many Yankee histories (he gave the priests, in particular, a good press). New England had its own inquisitions, he reminded his readers: witness the Salem witch trials. While the Irish were dying of famine, where were American troops? Off invading Catholic Mexico.[31]

Southern textbook authors got in their digs at northerners. They pointed out New England's superstition and cruelty in the witch trials, declared its weather nasty and cold, accused Yankees of harboring prejudice, and said they lied about slavery and the Civil War. One writer justified the slave economy by arguing that it was the "steady and directed toil of the South [that] first placed the United States among the great commercial nations of the world." Even in mathematics and rhetoric the Confederate textbooks put down the North.[32]

After the Civil War many states and territories banned "sectarian" and "partisan" textbooks by law at about the same time that they required all children and teachers to study history. The states did not mean to mandate just any form of history; they wanted correct history. Northern Republicans, pressured by veterans' organizations, expected children to learn the Civil War according to the version favored by the Grand Army of the Republic. In the South, Confederate veterans and Democratic legislatures also banned partisan teaching (the northern version). States subsidized new textbooks that would tell their own truth about the Confederacy and Reconstruction. In an act to secure "a Correct History of the United States," Florida declared that "no book called History, which does not tell the truth or withholds it, is worthy of the name or should be taught in public schools."[33]

Southerners and northerners, Protestants and Catholics—all had their own versions of "real" history. They were hardly relativists. Each religion and region wanted its own people to be represented in a favorable light in the school histories, not ignored or degraded. Nineteenth-century critics of textbooks typically were white, middle-class, male patriots—much like the authors—who believed that school histories should tell of heroism, loyalty, and progress. They still wanted to teach about explorers, military campaigns, the founding fathers, and the succession of Presidents and their administrations. They wanted to amend real history, not transform it.

Americans All?

Nineteenth-century textbook writers found that being nonpartisan and nonsectarian in textbooks was not so simple in practice as it was in theory. Religion, race, and region had proven to be disturbers of the peace in patriotic pedagogy; another R, radicalism, came to be added to the thesaurus of anxiety about the fate of the nation.

At the turn of the twentieth century, attention shifted to a major challenge: how to use school histories to "Americanize" immigrants. During World War I and its aftermath, groups such as the American Legion, the Daughters of the American Revolution, the American Bar Association, and federal agencies had a feeding frenzy of patriotism. They worried that immigrants and their children were underexposed to traditional patriotic history and in danger of subversion by radicals. The federal government commissioned its own Americanization textbooks and encouraged schools and churches and factories to turn the strangers into citizens. The American Bar Association lobbied legislatures to require teachers and students to study the Constitution. By and large the 100-percent Americans wanted to preserve—and strengthen—the kind of "real history" that had dominated texts in the nineteenth century. History was too important to be left to the historians, who kept on dreaming up new and fishy interpretations of familiar events. In the 1920s a number of states prohibited American history textbooks that criticized the heroes celebrated in real history. Oregon, for example, made it illegal to use any textbook that "speaks slightingly of the founders of the republic, or of the men who preserved the union, or which belittles or undervalues their work." History could not be, in this scheme of things, both critical and patriotic.[34]

A major change appeared in some of the school histories during

World War I, however. Eager to enlist history in the war effort, text-book authors rewrote historical texts to illustrate the evils of America's foes, the Huns, and the virtues of America's allies, the English. Irish and German ethnic associations attacked this new history as un-American because it exalted the British. It was false, they said, for it violated what Americans knew from their school histories. After all, had not the United States defeated the English in two wars? Critics attacked one historian because he had written that the British had "returned courageously to the attack." Tongue in cheek, he edited his textbook to say that "three times the cowardly British" went back to battle.[35]

The American Legion attacked Anglophile textbooks and de-cided to commission its own enthusiastic author. The Irish enjoyed twisting the English lion's tail, and the German-Americans, who had suffered persecution and ostracism during the war, mobilized in groups like the Steuben Society of America to set the historical record straight. The Knights of Columbus, an organization that spoke out for immigrant groups, also protested the Anglo-conformity required by the Americanizers. The National Association for the Advancement of Colored People led the attack on textbook dis-tortions and omissions concerning the history of blacks.[36]

In her study of high school textbooks in American history Micheline Fedyck shows that high school textbook discussions of "older immigrants" from northwestern Europe—the Germans, Scotch-Irish, and English in particular—were mostly favorable. These new-comers knew and appreciated democracy, rapidly became citizens, and were "racially" similar to the nation's Anglo-Saxon stock. By contrast, the "new" immigrants from southeastern Europe were of-ten portrayed in the textbooks in derogatory and racist terms dur-ing the World War I period. They were a bad lot—illiterate, clannish, undemocratic, unintelligent. Many came here only to make money at menial jobs and then return to the old country. Since the Civil

War, said one text in 1921, most immigrants "have been from the lower classes . . . and they give much trouble. They are for the most part very ignorant, and having been downtrodden in their old homes, they have no respect for law or government. In fact, many of them would like to see the government of the United States destroyed. How to deal with this undesirable class of immigrants is one of the most serious problems that we have today."[37] "Would it be possible," asked another school history, "to absorb the millions of olive-skinned Italians, and swarthy, black-haired Slavs, and dark-eyed Hebrews into the body of the American people?" It is evidence of their own clannishness that the Anglo-Saxon textbook writers did not worry much about the effect of such slurs on immigrant students or their families.[38]

But Fedyck found that by the 1930s and 1940s the southeastern Europeans had been transformed in the textbooks: They contributed to trade, literature, art, entertainment, banking, and scientific research. They did the hard work of mines, mills, and construction. If they sometimes fell behind in the American march of economic and social progress, that was often because they were treated badly.[39]

This shift in textbook assessments of European immigrant groups in the 1930s and 1940s fit an "Americans-All" model of ethnic assimilation (discussed in Chapter 3). Instead of trying—usually unsuccessfully—to "Americanize" newcomers by draconian means, educators came to prefer an add-and-stir model. The real history of the republic was still mostly a narrative of white men pursuing politics and wars, but other groups were incorporated into the narrative when appropriate—as, for example, mentions of soldiers from other lands who defended America. By the 1940s it had become acceptable to be hyphenated (a Polish-American, for example) but only if one stressed the *American* side of the hyphen.

It is of course very difficult to assess how immigrant students reacted to the school history taught in the texts. Still, contrasting views of texts by two pupils suggest a range of reactions from pleasure in citizenship to anger over gratuitous insult. The Jewish immigrant Mary Antin recalled her awe in reading aloud about her "Fellow Citizen" George Washington: "Never had I prayed . . . in such utter reverence and worship as I repeated the simple sentences of my child's story of the patriot. I gazed with adoration at the portraits of George and Martha Washington, till I could see them with my eyes shut." Antin could be loyal to both Moses and Washington. She might have been at home in the Hebrew Institute in New York, where students read the text of the Declaration of Independence in two parallel columns, one in English and one in Hebrew.[40]

But such direct blending of loyalties was unlikely for Guadalupe Toro Valdez, a Mexican-American student in a Texas school in 1919. In history class he and his fellow students were expected to read and recite the glories of the Texas Revolution and the exploits of Sam Houston in defeating Mexican soldiers and grabbing Mexican land. The Mexican-American students rebelled, defacing the pictures of Houston and then tearing the offending pages out of the textbooks. The next day as the teacher called on each one to recite, only to find the same pages missing, she "glanced at her own copy," Valdez recalled. "Watching her, the class was so still you could hear the specks of dust dancing on the sheaf of sunbeams that poured in through a window. Finally, red as a beet, she nodded her head and said, 'Let us take the next chapter for tomorrow. Class is dismissed.'"[41]

Even when they became more pluralistic in their choice of heroes, relatively few textbook writers raised questions about the justice and progress of American society or about its traditional heroes. When writers sometimes did cast a critical eye on basic institutions, as Harold Rugg did in his texts, they invited assault by the loyalty police. Rugg wrote an influential series of social studies textbooks that took a view of the "Americanization of America" very different from the Anglo-centered views of most 1920s texts. He saw Americanism as the enlargement of social justice, welcomed cultural diversity as a virtue not a threat, and adopted a more inclusive concept of citizenship that championed the underdog and the outsider. Rugg's broad definition of Americanism and his left-liberal views on the economy made him a favored target of conservatives in the Hearst Press, various business organizations, and patriotic societies. They effectively destroyed the market for his liberal textbooks. When Senator Joseph McCarthy tried in the 1950s to root out subversive people and subversive ideas, in education and elsewhere, he had plenty of precedent.[42]

In the 1960s and 1970s social movements in education came primarily from the left of the political spectrum, but the right has become increasingly vocal in recent decades. In the last generation social conservatives and religious groups have mounted powerful campaigns to restore prayer and Bible reading, to rid the schools of textbooks that advocate "secular humanism," and to give public funds to sectarian schools. As Zimmerman has argued, "many members of the Right have embraced pluralism and 'multiculturalism' in an effort to promote their own allegedly distinct or even threatened culture."[43]

Social movements have fueled new kinds of research in social history. Once marginal as fields of inquiry, African-American and women's history have entered the mainstream of historical scholarship. The history of immigration, of activist religious groups, and of the working class have also enjoyed a resurgence. Now those who wish to develop a pluralistic approach to the teaching of American history have rich resources on which to draw.[44]

In recent decades, this historical research and critiques by protest groups have expanded—and challenged—traditional notions of public truth in the school history textbooks. Groups such as women and blacks previously excluded from a narrative about white male politicians and military leaders have insisted that they be seen and heard in the textbooks, part of a larger public truth of oppression and achievement suppressed for too long in civic education. They called for far more than an additive model. Familiar historical episodes or actors were transformed when seen through the lenses of race and gender. What was true history now?[45]

Traditionally sensitive to criticism, not to say timid about it, textbook publishers have rapidly added images and stories about women and minorities. Scholars and activists have complained, however, that previously excluded groups have appeared not as main characters in the narrative but as figures in sidebars and illustrations. Surveys of high school textbooks have generally found that the development of the nation-state is still the master narrative in most books.[46]

Still, there are enough changes in textbook truths to upset traditionalists. In the early 1970s a Jules Feiffer cartoon expressed the annoyance and puzzlement of a white hard-hat worker about what had happened to the old certainties he had learned in school. Look at the strange new world his son met in his school history:

> When I went to school I learned that George Washington never told a lie, slaves were happy on the plantation, the men who opened the West were giants, and we won every war because God was on our side. But where my kid goes to school he learns that Washington was a slave-owner, slaves hated slavery, the men who opened the West committed genocide, and the wars we won were victories for U.S. imperialism. No wonder my kid's not an American. They're teaching him some other country's history.[47]

The old tale of political progress in the standard textbooks no longer seemed at all self-evident. Still, the familiar icons have in fact not disappeared, as the naturalization quiz and Buffalo students and U.S. senators suggest. School history has been more than a splash of words and pictures on the page. It was expected to make sense of the nation's origins and destiny. But that sense of real history, despite its apparently comforting coherence, was also a patchwork of ironies and contradictions and insults and omissions. The present history wars are a new chapter in an old book, an attempt to discover how citizens can respect their differences and search for common ground.[48]

Whither History Textbooks?

A history textbook today is hardly the republican catechism that Noah Webster appended to his famous speller. It is more like pieces of a sprawling novel with diverse characters and fascinating subplots waiting for an author to weave them into a broader narrative. Now a noisy confusion reigns about what stories the textbooks should tell. Special-interest groups of the right and left pressure publishers to include or drop topics, especially in big states such as California or Texas. Worries abound about old truths betrayed and new truths ignored. Many groups want to vet or veto what children learn, and it is unclear what roles teachers, parents, ethnic groups, religious activists, historians, and others should play. Tempers rise. In New York debates over a multicultural curriculum, Catherine Cornbleth and Dexter Waugh observed, "both sides engaged in a rhetoric of crisis, doom, and salvation."[49]

In the United States, unlike most other nations, private agencies—publishing companies—create and sell textbooks. Thus commerce plays an important part in deciding which historical truths shall be

official. To be sure, public agencies usually decide which textbooks
to adopt (about half of the states delegate text adoption to local districts, and the rest use some form of state adoption). For all the con-
ventionality of the product, the actual production and sale of
textbooks is still a risky business. It's very expensive to create and
print textbooks, and the market (the various agencies that actually
decide which to adopt) is somewhat unpredictable. In addition, at
any time some citizens are likely to protest whatever messages the
texts send. Textbook adoption can be a free-for-all.[50]

Thus it is not surprising that textbooks still beget textbooks. To
control risk, companies find it wise to copy successes. Old icons
(Washington) remain, but publishers respond to new demands by
multiplying new state-approved truths. It has been easier to add
those ubiquitous sidebars to the master narrative than to rethink it,
easier to incorporate new content into a safe and profitable for-
mula than to create new accounts. American history textbooks are
enormous—888 pages, on average—in part because publishers seek
to neutralize or anticipate criticisms by adding topics. The result is
often not comprehensive coverage but a bloated book devoid of
style or coherence.[51]

The traditional American fear of centralized power, salient today
in debates over national standards and tests, has resulted in a
strange patchwork of agencies and associations—textbook companies, state and local governments, lobby groups of many persuasions, individuals who want to play Grand Inquisitor—to choose
and monitor the public truths taught in the texts. One of the most
rapid ways of changing what students learn in American schools is
to transform the textbooks, but the present Rube Goldberg system
of creating and selecting textbooks makes such a change very difficult (though fine history textbooks have on occasion appeared).[52]

What are some strategies to cope with the cross-cutting demands on history textbooks? Three possible ones are these: muddling through with modest improvements; turning over the task of writing textbooks to experts; or devising texts that depart from the model of state-approved truths and embrace instead the taking of multiple perspectives. Each of these has some advantages and faults that are worth contemplating.

Muddling through may seem sensible to people who believe that there is a vast gap between superheated policy talk about the defects of textbooks and the everyday reality teachers face in classrooms. Is all the debate over bad textbooks a dust-devil masquerading as a tornado? For many teachers, the big challenge is to prepare students for high-stakes tests they must take for graduation, and textbooks are a key resource in that task.[53]

Teachers tend to find the status quo in textbooks more bearable than do the critics. When a sample of classroom teachers was asked their opinion of the textbooks they used, they generally said that the books are good and getting better. Teachers rely heavily on textbooks in their instruction, employing them for about 70 percent of class time.[54]

A commonsense argument for muddling through, with gradual improvement of textbooks, is that pedagogical reforms rarely work well if they are imposed on teachers. Study after study has shown that teachers tend to avoid controversy in teaching American history (indeed, being "nonpartisan" is still judged a virtue, as it was in the past). And parents and school board members, like teachers, have their own ideas about what is "real history." Too sharp a turn in the historical highway might topple reform. So some teachers argue that the best way to improve education is to keep the old icons and welcome the newcomers in the textbooks. And hope that the students in fact *do read* the textbooks! Common sense—that's the way to cope amid all the confusion.

An alternate approach to reform of textbooks is to set good state or local standards for history courses and turn the writing of textbooks over to experts—an approach used in many nations and sometimes advocated in the United States today. Muddling through just maintains the status quo and guarantees incoherence in textbooks and hence in learning. In the current politics and commerce of text publishing, "truth" becomes whatever the special interests (left or right) pressure textbook companies to say. Current textbooks are often victims of commercial timidity, veto groups, and elephantiasis (888 pages!).[55]

What is missing, proponents of this view argue, is a clear set of national standards about what students should know and a vivid and cogent text that engages students in learning. Those who call for expertise suggest that history is too important *not* to be left to the historians.

But this response to the faults of history texts presents its own problems. Calling in the experts doesn't eliminate disputes; Ph.D.s love to differ among themselves. Teachers are adept at sabotaging reforms dropped on them from above. And amid all the commercialism and special interests now rife in the process of selecting textbooks, the public still deserves some say in deciding what American students learn about the past, expert or not.

Patricia Nelson Limerick, professor of history at the University of Colorado, suggests a pluralistic model of history that contrasts with both muddling through and textbooks by experts. She recently suggested that the Little Bighorn Battlefield, where Sioux and Cheyenne fought George Armstrong Custer, needed not two monuments, one in honor of the Indians and one to recognize Custer and his soldiers, but "a different kind of memorial—one in which no point of view dominates." She imagines visitors walking among memorials to the warriors and Custer, but also to the enlisted men dragooned into the slaughter, to Custer's widow, to the families of the white soldiers, and to the children and wives of the Indian warriors.[56]

Such perspective-taking lies at the core of historical understanding of a socially diverse nation. Pluralistic history can enhance ethnic self-respect and empathy for other groups. Parallel to the monuments Limerick proposes, texts for a pluralistic civic education might have not one master narrative but several, capturing separate identities and experiences.

But the history of Americans in their separate groups would be partial without looking as well at their lives in interaction. Our society is pluralistic in character, and so should be the history we teach to young citizens. But alongside that *pluribus* citizens have also sought an *unum,* a set of shared political aspirations and institutions. One reason there have been so many textbook wars is that group after group has, in turn, sought to become part of a common story told about our past. The *unum* and the *pluribus* have been in inescapable tension, constantly evolving as Americans struggled to find common ground and to respect their differences.[57]

PART TWO

DIVERSITY

CHAPTER THREE

Same or Different?
School Policies and Social Diversity

THIS chapter began in conversations with Paul Vass and Gus Barros, two immigrants from the Cape Verde Islands, Portuguese colonies located about three hundred miles from the west coast of Africa. The three of us worked alongside each other as construction laborers. We talked as we dug ditches and lugged two-by-fours and ate lunch in the shade of a sycamore tree on hot August days. They introduced me to their community in Roxbury, Massachusetts.

That was fifty years ago, but the experience is still vivid. Their accounts of their lives and their puzzlement about America raised questions I have since pondered. Long before I had heard about the "social construction of reality," Paul and Gus taught me how arbitrary and punitive was the American conception and practice of "race." In the Cape Verde Islands, people did make distinctions between individuals based on appearance—indeed, they used some two hundred and fifty categories to describe one another, according to one anthropologist. But the United States was different: there people came, it seemed, in two varieties, black and white. One "drop of Negro blood" and you were Negro, said law and custom in a deeply racist society.[1]

Authorities—sergeants, school principals, immigration officers, census takers, doctors—expected Cape Verdeans to declare on which side of the color line they belonged. Government policed the categories and boundaries called "race." Two brown-skinned Cape Verdean men, brothers, told me that when they were drafted, a sergeant at Fort Devens ordered all Negroes to take two steps forward; then he commanded them to march off to segregated units. One brother stayed put and went through World War II as a white soldier; the other stepped ahead and joined a black unit.

In the Islands and in America, among their families and friends, Cape Verdeans spoke a creole language that mixed Portuguese and African tongues. They identified themselves as immigrants from Fogo or Brava, as islanders with distinctive folkways. They migrated voluntarily to find work or avoid drought-induced famine while seeking ways to preserve their culture. Generally, they did not think of themselves as African-Americans, whatever their skin color. They were shunned by Portuguese immigrants from the Azores who wanted to be considered white and who typically cold-shouldered Cape Verdeans in their Azorean churches, schools, neighborhoods, and social clubs.

The Cape Verdeans I came to know in 1951–52 taught me that although there may not be something called "race," there surely was something called racism, and it was absurd and cruel in the way it shaped their lives. Even though the dominant conception of race made no sense as science, the color line counted. Whites believed themselves entitled to most of the good schools, good jobs, political power, opportunity for higher education, and cultural recognition and legitimacy.

As a historian of American education, I have continued to be fascinated by the many ways in which Americans have construed human sameness and diversity as they built systems of public schooling.

Schools have sometimes adopted a policy of treating all children alike. Liberal educators of the 1950s tried to be color blind since equality to them meant sameness of treatment. Good schools were supposed to mold good citizens according to a common moral and civic pattern.[2]

But counter to a creed of color-blind equality and fairness ran a relentless human urge to discriminate by classification, to stratify plants into weeds and flowers, dogs into purebreds and mongrels, and people into superior and inferior "races." Many groups have wanted to preserve or create their own place in the sun and have contended with one another for advantage in education as in other domains. Educational institutions themselves have generated new categories of persons who were winners or losers, as I explore in the next chapter.

In the kaleidoscopic last half of the twentieth century many people came to question whether treating all students alike was either possible or desirable. The social differences that liberals of the 1950s had tried to play down took stage center in the new politics of diversity of the 1960s and 1970s. The media highlighted the contentious issues that arose: racial desegregation, bilingual instruction, Bible reading, multicultural curriculums, new gender policies and practices, sex education, separate Afro-centric academies, prayer in the schools, and so it went. Clashing social values brought both hope and disillusionment. The civil rights movement, the war half a world away in Vietnam, an activist Supreme Court, and social movements like feminism all influenced school policies.[3]

Older conceptions of race, gender, and ethnicity that once were taken for granted as part of the "natural" and essential order in society have become subjects of intense scrutiny and controversy. For decades census categories used to classify Americans have become emotionally charged. Increasingly, people have become aware of the arbitrariness of the social construction of human differences. That puts the very concept of social "difference" on a slippery slope. What differences do count in education and why? Which are important but neglected in policymaking? Economic class, for example, is an important form of difference, but it has been downplayed, despite growing gaps in income and wealth.[4]

It is easier to devise fashionable slogans about diversity in education than to develop coherent and just policies in schools. The historical conflicts, compromises, retreats, advances, contradictions, and triumphs evident in the schools' encounter with social diversity persist into the present and pose an intellectual as well as a practical challenge to those who seek social justice today. A place to start in understanding policies on diversity is to compare the social constructions of "race," "gender," and "ethnicity," and to explore the educational policies linked to these forms of social diversity.

Social Constructions of Diversity

Conceptions of social differences often spin complex meanings from supposedly natural distinctions between people. "The problem with this language of difference," Michael Katz observes, "is both philosophic and practical. We assume that verbal distinctions reflect natural or inherent qualities of people . . . for reasons of convenience, power, or moral judgment, we select from among a myriad of traits and then sort people, objects, and situations into categories which we then treat as real." That's the problem: Invidious distinctions produce injustice. This creates a dilemma, notes Martha Minow: "How to overcome the past hostilities and degradations of people on the basis of group differences without employing . . . those very differences." One may deplore and demolish, for example, the notion that some "races" are inferior, but in order to correct the educational injustices justified by that concept, one must at the same time pay attention to the many ways racism has structured opportunity and exploitation.[5]

Concepts of racial inferiority have formed what Horace Mann Bond called "a crazy-quilt world of unreality" in a society that proclaimed equality, opportunity, and democracy as goals while it "brutalized, degraded, and dehumanized" African-Americans "by every instrument of the culture." During World War II, for example, the racial caste system of the South made it seem natural that white Nazi prisoners of war on their way to a prison camp in Texas should eat their meal inside a "whites only" dining room in a railroad station while their black American guards waited outside.[6]

Concepts of gender give another illustration of cultural constructions of social difference. By "gender" I mean the cultural meanings people have attached to the biological differences between the sexes. Over time and place humans have given a vast array of interpretations to these biological differences; there is no one "natural" way of being male or female. Societies deal in different ways with persons who are biologically not of one sex, hermaphrodites. The anthropologist Clifford Geertz reports that in some cultures intersexed people are honored as wise counselors, in others killed as demons, and in the contemporary United States regarded as medical anomalies to be fixed by surgeons.[7]

However fanciful some traditional conceptions of gender may be, they customarily have assured that men would remain in charge. In the United States, the cash value of beliefs about gender is evident in the fact that in the mid-twentieth century employed white women earned on average about three fifths of the income of white men.[8]

Americans have construed ethnic differences in a variety of ways over time. Successive surges of immigrants, speaking dozens of lan-

guages and representing many traditions, have raised the question
of how schools should deal with different cultures. Ardent "Americanizers" defined immigrants, especially those from southeastern
Europe, as strangers, as potentially dangerous "aliens" who must become "naturalized" (an odd word in this context). They must accept the values and leadership of whites born in this country—the
so-called native-born. The optimists among the Americanizers believed that ethnicity could be shed like a cloak. The pessimists believed that the differences between the newcomer ethnic groups
and themselves were hereditary and that immigration should be
curbed. But both optimists and pessimists believed that unassimilated ethnic groups posed a threat.

Advocates of cultural pluralism, by contrast, glorified ethnic diversity and sometimes called on immigrants to retain their "Old
World traits" intact as if they were timeless heirlooms. Sameness
once again warred with difference in educational policy. Both the
Americanizers and the pluralists, however, posed misleading
choices.

In American society the boundaries between groups have been
highly permeable. Cultural influences have moved every which
way, affecting both the newcomers and the old-time Americans.
Immigrants discovered their "otherness" in the process of immigration and the self-conscious process of adapting to a new land. The
various nationalities now lumped together as "Europeans" hardly
thought of themselves as one homogeneous group. Serbs and
Croats, southern and northern Italians, French and Germans, Irish
Catholics and Irish Protestants did not forget their traditional hostilities when they stepped off the boat.[9]

Any one person—say a black, middle-class, Catholic woman who
was a teacher—might have a mixture of identities that were salient
in different ways in different contexts. As Henry Louis Gates, Jr.,

observes, "Pluralism isn't supposed to be about policing boundaries. It's supposed to be about breaking those boundaries down,
and acknowledging the fluid nature of all identities." The groups
composing American society have shaped themselves and one another as they interacted, but in influencing educational policies
they did not compete on a level playing field.[10]

During the last century most of the prominent policymakers in
public education and most administrators of public school systems
have been U.S. born, white, prosperous, male, and Protestant. As
"mainstream" leaders, they have generally assumed that their own
beliefs about social diversity were authoritative. Indeed, often they
took their civic and moral outlooks for granted, at least until these
cultural constructions were challenged politically. They surely did not
think of themselves simply as one group among many (nonbrown,
nonfemale, nonimmigrant, non-poor). Instead they saw themselves
as the quintessential Americans. The "others," however—immigrants,
African-Americans, Catholics, Jews, females, Asians, and similar
groups—have hardly been content to be wax on which leaders
stamped their educational imprint.[11]

School Policies toward European Immigrants

In 1891 leaders in the National Education Association (NEA) declared that all children should be compelled to attend schools
whose classes were taught in English. They feared that "foreign influence has begun a system of colonization with a purpose of preserving foreign languages and traditions and proportionately of
destroying distinctive Americanism." Demanding compulsory Americanization, one educator asserted that "when the people established
this government they had a certain standard of intelligence and
morality"; once Americans could assume "that an intelligent and

moral people will conform to the requirements of good citizenship." By the 1890s, he warned, this outlook could no longer be taken for granted: "People have come here who are not entitled to freedom in the same sense as those who established this government." It was unthinkable "to lower this idea of intelligence and morality to the standard" of the newcomers.[12]

The NEA leaders spoke during a turning point when elites were seeking to draw sharp contrasts between the "old" immigrants from northwestern Europe, who presumably were easily assimilated to an "American" mold, and the "new," who supposedly did not fit the native pattern of citizenship. By then the immigrants pouring in massive numbers into American cities were Italians, Poles, Russians, and others from southeastern Europe who were mostly Catholic or Jewish.

Already apparent in the NEA discussion were some central themes in the nativist construction of ethnic difference. The "new" immigrants, inferior in intelligence and civic morality, were clustering in "foreign colonies." People who still had faith in the power of education thought it possible to meet the emergency by compelling the children of immigrants to attend public schools, learn English, and be deliberately inculcated with American political and cultural values. Skeptics said the problem was beyond the reach of the school; they quoted social scientists who supposedly proved the inferiority of the southeastern European "races" and who insisted that the nation could be saved only by forbidding, or severely limiting, immigration to American shores.[13]

The restriction of immigration did not solve the problem of what to do with the people already here. In 1909 about three fifths of the students in the nation's thirty-seven largest cities had foreign-born parents. No longer, thought Anglo reformers, could schools go about business as usual. It was necessary to catch all the newcomer children in the net. The child was coming to belong more to the state and less to the parents, leading educators believed, and the state's interest and duty were to educate the immigrant child to be an American. Underlying most attempts at "Americanization," as Michael Olneck has pointed out, was a "symbolic delegitimation of collective ethnic identity," and this became deliberate state policy.[14]

Early in the twentieth century leading educators agreed on the goal of assimilating immigrants but differed on the best means of accomplishing that task. Some urged a sharp-edged intervention: In order to assimilate a motley collection of humanity, schools should drive a wedge between students and their parental culture and language, thereby capturing the second generation. Humanitarian reformers who knew immigrant families first hand—for example, settlement house workers and child labor inspectors—recognized the pain this confrontational strategy could bring. As I discuss in Chapter 4, they wanted to give children health care, free lunches, and counseling, and they sought to match schools better to the cultural backgrounds of immigrants so that assimilation could be gentle and gradual rather than painful and abrupt.[15]

Many reformers active in urban school reform believed that newcomer children needed compensatory socialization that went well beyond traditional forms of cognitive instruction. Immigrant children, like their parents in adult Americanization classes, learned about proper sanitation and health and "American" styles of eating and dressing. Even recreation had a patriotic flavor, and learning proper use of leisure hours became one of the Seven Cardinal Principles of Secondary Education adopted by the National Education Association. Nothing should be left to chance in the socialization of immigrants.[16]

Although there was a constitutional separation of church and state, which helped to protect the religious core of immigrant cultures from state action, Americanizers did not believe that there should be a separation of ethnicity and state. Thus the state could not persecute Baptists but could attempt to denationalize German immigrants. There was no bill of rights for cultural diversity. Increasingly, the state reached into the family, for example compelling children to attend school for more and more years, in part so that the children of immigrants would have more time in school to become American. Underlying most attempts at "Americanization" was a desire to replace European ethnic identity with a new identity as an individual U.S. citizen. When World War I broke out, eradication of competing cultural allegiances became deliberate educational policy.[17]

World War I brought to a boil nativist anxiety about "foreign colonies" and a fifth column of unassimilated aliens within the nation. For a time the hard-edged Americanizers dominated policy. The Red Scare and nativist organizations kept paranoia alive well into the 1920s. Employers, churches, federal and state bureaus, patriotic associations, and many other organizations joined forces with public schools to eradicate "hyphenism" among foreign-born adults and to ensure that their children were exposed to the same politically correct civic instruction. John Dewey attacked this frenzy for conformity in 1916 when he said that "such terms as Irish-American or Hebrew-American or German-American are false terms because they seem to assume something which is already in existence called American, to which the other factor may be externally hitcht [sic] on. The fact is, the genuine American, the typical American, is himself a hyphenated character."[18]

Groups such as the American Legion, the American Bar Association, and the Daughters of the American Revolution pressured dozens of states to pass laws prescribing the teaching of American history and the Constitution. Although only one state required the

teaching of "citizenship" in 1903, by 1923 thirty-nine did so. The
National Security League lobbied to ban the teaching of German
and to prescribe super-patriotic instruction. Thanks in part to its efforts, thirty-three states mandated that all teachers pass a test on the
Constitution in order to be certified. By 1923 thirty-five states had
enacted legislation that made English the only language of instruction in public schools. In Oregon in 1922 the Ku Klux Klan, which
treated the little red schoolhouse as a symbol of Americanism, lobbied successfully for a law mandating that all children attend public schools.[19]

Anything foreign was suspect. In New York City, schoolchildren
who went into the tenements to sell war bonds were instructed to
report adults whose loyalty was dubious. The campaign to define
"American" in a narrow conservative mold and to enforce conformity of thought and deed among immigrants outraged many
ethnic leaders, much of the ethnic press, and a number of U.S.-born
liberals. Despite threats and coercion, only a small minority of adult
immigrants enrolled in Americanization classes, and those who did
rarely completed the courses.[20]

In reaction to the hard-edged Americanizers, a few writers called
for ethnic self-preservation. In 1924, for example, Horace M. Kallen
proposed "a democracy of nationalities" in which all groups would
enhance "the selfhood which is inalienable in them, and for the re-
alization of which they require 'inalienable' liberty." Kallen argued
that culture was "ancestrally determined" rather than an interactive
and constantly changing set of practices: "Men may change their
clothes, their politics, their wives, their religion, their philosophies,
to a greater or lesser extent; they cannot change their grandpar-
ents." Public schools, he thought, should attempt not to stamp out
but rather to preserve ethnic "self-realization through the perfection
of men according to their kind."[21]

Talk about total ethnic preservation or total assimilation bore little relation to the everyday lives of immigrant families, whose cultural practices blended the old and the new in kaleidoscopic ways. The newcomers were remarkably heterogeneous in economic class, formal schooling, religion, economic skills, political experience, and cultural and familial patterns.

No stereotype of "the immigrant" could capture such diversity. Some immigrants saw the public school as a gateway to economic opportunity. Others played down education and instead wanted their children to work to contribute to the family's long collaborative climb out of poverty. Ethnic and religious communities built their own institutions—churches, clubs, mutual benefit societies, and political organizations—as mediating structures that eased adaptation to American life while preserving valued traditions. The children of immigrants often learned American ways most powerfully not from teachers but from peers intolerant of cultural differences. In some communities youths rejected the efforts of elders in their ethnic groups to preserve the language and traditions of the old country. Aspirations and alienation crisscrossed the lives of immigrant families, only dimly understood by many of the educators who sought to assimilate them.[22]

The frenzy of nativism during World War I and its aftermath turned "Americanization" into yet another pedagogical specialty, especially for writers of civics texts and educators of adults. Public schools became accountable for producing patriots. A good proportion of the experts in "Americanization," however, deplored paranoid ideology and harsh methods. After laws in 1921 and 1924 restricted immigration, educators thought that they could go about assimilating the second generation at a less frenetic pace. Social scientists began to portray assimilation as a long-term and complex intergenerational process. "In the eyes of many liberals," Nicholas V. Montalto writes, "the Americanization movement epitomized all that was wrong in the American attitude and policy toward the immigrant: the bankruptcy of racism and chauvinism, the tendency to blame the immigrant for domestic social problems, and the failure of coercion."[23]

These liberal professionals, many of whom were second-generation immigrants themselves, believed that attacks solidified ethnic groups rather than dissolving them. Denigrating the language and cultures of students' parents, they argued, split apart families and created an alienated second generation that was neither foreign nor American. Increasingly these specialists in assimilation argued that a more tolerant, slow-paced approach would produce better results than high-pressure methods. They still thought that the public schools should "Americanize" pupils, but they wanted transitional programs that taught tolerance for diversity and preached the doctrine that the United States was a composite of the contributions of many nations. For their part, activist groups of Irish and German immigrants insisted on textbooks that honored their ethnic contributions to the patriotic mainstream of American history.[24]

Many schools and other organizations serving immigrants sponsored pageants, dances, plays, and ethnic feasts that stressed the "gifts" made by immigrants to American society. They celebrated differences while ultimately working toward assimilation—a strategy of gradual transition rather than forced Americanization. In the 1920s and 1930s, some progressive educators experimented with forms of cross-cultural learning. Polish pupils in Toledo, Ohio, for example, studied their parents' history and culture; students in Neptune, New Jersey, created ethnic family trees and learned the history of their ancestors; in Santa Barbara, California, pupils prepared exhibits on Chinese art, Scandinavian crafts, and Pacific cultures; and Mexican children in Phoenix, Arizona, attended a class, taught in Spanish, on Mexican history and culture.[25]

The best-articulated version of this early form of pluralism in education appeared in the 1930s in the "intercultural education" movement led by Rachel Davis DuBois, a Quaker and former teacher (no relation to the black scholar and activist W. E. B. Du Bois). In 1924 she inaugurated, in Woodbury High School in southern New Jersey, a series of student assemblies on the achievements of different ethnic groups, pioneering in a practice that was to become a hallmark of her career. As she expanded her work, she enlisted powerful allies: progressive educators at Teachers College, Columbia, leaders of ethnic organizations, and social scientists concerned with intergroup relations.[26]

Although this was a disparate coalition, most of the activists in the intercultural education movement agreed on some basic goals and policies. They wanted to dispel prejudices and stereotypes that might trigger a new burst of nativism and intergroup violence during the hard times of the Great Depression and later the turmoil of World War II. They were concerned about what Louis Adamic called "Thirty Million New Americans," the youthful second generation suspended between two worlds, a group described by the sociologist Robert Park as "footloose, prowling and predacious." They believed that an appreciation for the traditions of the parents would bridge the family gap and help the second generation to find a productive adjustment to American society. They agreed that all Americans, those "on the hill" as well as those "across the tracks," needed better knowledge of one another in order to establish social harmony. By "cultural democracy" they meant fair play for individuals from all groups, self-respect, and appreciation for diversity.[27]

DuBois and key supporters of the intercultural movement disagreed about an important strategy, however, as Montalto has documented. DuBois thought that each ethnic group should be studied in a separate unit rather than having teachers mix them together. Only in this manner, she thought, would children of immigrants and minorities be able to acquire a positive self-conception and thereby cure "the alienation, rootlessness, and emotional disorders afflicting the second generation." Psychic strength would result from strong positive identification with one's ethnic group.[28]

Influential colleagues in the movement dissented, especially members of the Progressive Education Association and many of the social scientists associated with intercultural education. One critic dismissed her argument about self-esteem as "compensatory idealized tradition," and many were worried that the separate approach would solidify ethnic islands and increase, not diminish, group conflict. On the eve of World War II, a time of heightened concern about national unity, two superintendents said that DuBois's curriculum would "arouse in the thinking of so-called minority groups an undesirable emphasis upon their own importance and a determination to insist upon their own rights." What they wanted was an intercultural strategy that would use psychological methods to preserve civic peace, not mobilize dissidents to secure their rights.[29]

Michael Olneck has observed that most educators—the hard-line Americanizers and the interculturalists alike—distrusted collective ethnic identities. In civics texts and the writings of the interculturalists, he has identified an underlying ideology of individualism and an ideal of including all people, as individuals, in a greater unity called American society. The cure for group conflict was understanding and appreciation; over time this approach would result in the inclusion of members of all groups in the mainstream of society as autonomous individuals. Oppression became reduced to stereotyping, and separate ethnic identity was to be dissolved as painlessly as possible. Being a good citizen meant doing one's everyday duties more than taking part actively in politics.[30]

Professional educators founded and led the intercultural education movement of the 1930s and 1940, and various ethnic organizations and individuals lent important support. In recent times much of the energy behind "multicultural education" comes from grass-roots protest movements, from demands for inclusion of African-Americans, Hispanics, and other subordinated groups. Some activists saw that curricular change could go well beyond the addition of a few "contributions"; knowledge of how the group was unjustly treated and a better understanding of how to achieve equality could motivate members of groups to overcome subordination. Some also saw ethnic studies and bilingual-bicultural education as a way of preserving the distinctive cultures of groups, rather than as a step toward cultural assimilation.[31]

Thus a competing construction of pluralism began to emerge, one that suggested a goal of equality of groups as opposed to equality of individuals. It demanded a new definition of the public culture that did not simply celebrate cultural differences and then go on to prize a core of common values rooted in middle-class American individualism. The new version of pluralism was explicitly political and challenged not just the traditional academic canon but also entrenched interests that had sustained discrimination. Not surprisingly, this strategy has aroused far more controversy than earlier forms of intercultural education.[32]

School Policies toward People of Color

If *assimilation* was the keynote of policy for immigrants, *discrimination* was a basic theme of the education of people of color. Black, Japanese, and Chinese people were categorized as members of unassimilable and inferior "races." Until the *Brown* school desegregation decision in 1954, relatively few educators followed the lead of reformers like Horace Mann Bond, W. E. B. Du Bois, or Rachel

DuBois, who demanded a frontal assault on racism in school and society. The story was different with European immigrants. Although some educational policymakers dismissed southeastern European newcomers as people of "inferior stock," most believed that all white ethnics could be and must be absorbed into American society as soon as possible. They should become U.S. citizens who shared American rights and culture.

Black Americans, by contrast, often had to fight simply to gain access to public education and frequently had to build and staff their own schools. Whites tended to regard the schooling of blacks as a charity, not a common entitlement. In the South after the Civil War, blacks took the initiative in setting up schools for freed slaves, aided by northern missionaries and the Freedmen's Bureau. When southern whites gained control of public schools in the former Confederate states, partly by disenfranchising blacks, they used schools as a buttress of a caste system designed to subordinate blacks socially, to cramp them economically under a rigid job ceiling, and to deny them their political rights as citizens.[33]

Exclusion and segregation also characterized whites' treatment of "Mongolians." Congress banned Chinese immigrants, and some states, such as California, deprived Chinese and Japanese immigrants of many of the rights of citizenship, including the opportunity to send their children to public schools. Quintessential "strangers," these Asians were, like blacks, defined by descent and identified by their physical characteristics. Whites feared them as competitors for jobs, stereotyped them in vicious ways, and thought them incapable of ever becoming "Americans." When Asian groups formed their own supportive institutions and clustered in enclaves, these actions were interpreted as evidence of their clannishness. Isolated and feared as a domestic fifth column, Japanese-Americans were herded into detention centers during World War II at the very time when interculturalists were insisting that racial and ethnic discrimination was un-American.[34]

Another group that faced severe discrimination on grounds of color, but not only for that reason, was children of Mexican immigrants. They occupied an ambiguous "racial" status in a nation that had drawn sharp lines between "whites" and "Negroes." In Texas in the *Salvatierra* decision in 1930, persons of Mexican descent were declared members of the "white race" (in distinction to African-Americans, who were totally segregated from whites in that state), while in California that year the attorney general declared them to be "Indians" and hence subject to school segregation. But even where they were legally "white," legal decrees and the conventional wisdom of educators justified separating Mexican-Americans in school because they had distinctive "needs" and "traits." They were poor and often migratory; they spoke Spanish, not English; and they scored low on tests oriented to middle-class Anglos.[35]

Families of Mexican descent, usually impoverished and with little political power, were used as cheap labor when needed and deported when they were not. Denied the vote and migrating from place to place in search of work, Mexican-American farmworkers had little influence over the schooling of their children. In Texas in 1928, about 40 percent of Mexican children did not attend school, and of those that did, almost half were in the first grade. Educators frequently segregated them, assumed that they needed only a minimal education, and devoted few resources to their instruction. A Texas superintendent explained why: "Most of our Mexicans are of the lower class. They transplant onions, harvest them, etc. The less they know about everything else, the better contented they are. . . . If a man has very much sense or education either, he is not going to stick to this kind of work. So you see it is up to the white population to keep the Mexican on his knees in the onion patch."[36] In fact if not in law, Mexicans were often treated in schools as a separate "race."

The racial ideology of white supremacy defined people of color as nonassimilable, ineradicably different, and not, therefore, full citizens. An elaborate set of racist beliefs justified segregation, political subordination, hostile and demeaning stereotypes, and economic exploitation of people of color. To be born white was to have powerful advantages in the political and economic system and to dominate the public culture.[37]

How did white educational leaders respond to "the Negro problem"? This question is hard to answer, in part because of silence on the issue in many quarters. Educators talked a lot about assimilation of immigrants but little about the systematic discrimination against blacks. Policies on the education of blacks differed by region. In the South it was only the rare and courageous white educator who challenged the caste system in education, so embedded was white supremacy in the southern social order. Fearful of alienating its southern members, the major national educational association, the NEA, did not desegregate its southern branches until the 1960s (though the organization had long endorsed better "intergroup relations").[38]

In the North, blacks often faced less blatant but still powerful prejudice and institutional racism. The "science" of education, on which many educators relied in making decisions about students, was riddled with racist assumptions. Culturally biased IQ tests, whose defects were magnified by racist misinterpretations, seemed to justify relegating blacks to nonacademic tracks. "Realistic" views of the job market impelled counselors to steer blacks into manual work. Social differences that were the product of discrimination and poverty became validated as the way things "naturally" were. It is thus not surprising that when Ellwood P. Cubberley classified library books on Negroes, he put them on the shelf next to those on the "education of special classes" along with the blind, "retarded," and "crippled."[39]

Some individual educators and organizations did attack racism in education. The Intercultural Education Bureau, for example, sought to bring about greater understanding between blacks and whites. The favored approach was to attack social prejudices rather than mounting political and legal attacks on the institutional structures that held blacks down. It is probable, in any case, that only a small minority of white educational leaders from 1890 to 1954 openly confronted the racism embedded in American society and its system of public education.[40]

Blacks themselves, allied with this small minority of white educators and activists in other fields, took the lead in fighting the educational discrimination that was buttressed by the cultural construction of the "Negro race." Voteless in the South and pushed to the periphery in the North, blacks faced a cruel dilemma: to accept segregation was to ratify their status as noncitizens and to send their children to schools that were grossly unequal, but to enroll their children in desegregated white-dominated schools often meant denying teaching jobs to blacks, exposing their children to prejudiced whites, and failing to instill the self-respect that came from studying their own history and culture. W. E. B. Du Bois, a brilliant spokesman for social justice for African-Americans, argued at different times for both strategies.[41]

Horace Mann Bond recalled that in 1934 "racial segregation appeared to be an immutable feature of the American social order." The New Deal did not have a coherent educational or racial policy, and black schools in the South remained impoverished and segregated in the 1930s. But some activist New Dealers did find ways to assist African-Americans educationally through programs of employment and relief such as the National Youth Administration (NYA), the Works Progress Administration, and the Civilian Conservation Corps (even though the programs were frequently segregated). These experiments later served as precedents for 1960s programs in the War on Poverty (Lyndon B. Johnson had been a star NYA administrator in Texas during the Depression).[42]

When World War II arrived and acute manpower shortages appeared, the legacy of neglect of black education became apparent. About twice as many blacks as whites were rejected for the military, almost always because they failed "to meet minimum educational requirements." This meant that proportionally many more whites were drafted than blacks. In response, the army mounted a massive remedial literacy program to counteract the results of the starvation diet of schooling received by southern blacks for decades.[43]

By 1946 the National Association for the Advancement of Colored People had attracted nearly 450,000 members and was pressing the series of educational desegregation cases that culminated in the *Brown* decision in 1954. Even before *Brown* blacks had seen desegregation as a promise of full citizenship one day, a way to bring down the caste system. But the dilemma of segregation persisted, as W. E. B. Du Bois declared shortly after the Supreme Court spoke: blacks knew "what their children must suffer [in desegregated schools] for years from southern white teachers, from white hoodlums who sit beside them and under school authorities from janitors to superintendents who despise them." He warned that blacks could lose the opportunity to study their own history of resistance and achievement and "eventually surrender race solidarity and the idea of American Negro culture to the concept of world humanity, above race and nation. This is the price of liberty. This is the cost of oppression."[44]

At first, blacks bore the major burden of enforcing their own constitutional rights. Although de jure segregation was against the law, few local white leaders took the initiative in integrating school districts. Through sit-ins, demonstrations, boycotts, and strikes in countless local communities black activists and a few white allies challenged the old racial order. The battles brought slow progress: a decade after *Brown*, about nine out of ten southern black children still went to all-black schools. School desegregation picked up momentum in the South in the late 1960s as courts and the Civil Rights Act of 1964 increasingly put the weight of the federal government against de jure segregation and as southern blacks successfully pressed for the vote.[45]

Desegregation almost always meant opening white schools to blacks, not the reverse. One result in the South was the wholesale firing of black principals and the loss of the black schools as a center of African-American solidarity, as Dubois had predicted. The overwhelming majority of blacks indicated in polls that they favored desegregation, in part because it was so tied to their rights as citizens, especially in the South. They also knew that black schools had far fewer resources than white schools; perhaps if white children studied alongside blacks, as hostages, black students might finally receive a similar education. But in northern cities many blacks, dissatisfied with the glacial pace of desegregation, decided to push for their own community-controlled schools in which black staff would predominate and their children could study black culture. If they were going to continue to be defined by their "racial" status, then they, and not whites, should be in charge of their children's education.[46]

On the surface the community control movement conflicted with the color-blind ideology of *Brown* and of liberal integrationists. Underneath both the desegregation and community-control strategies, however, was a common aim of blacks: better education for their children in a society in which institutional racism, if not caste, was still a powerful force.[47]

When black activists pushed in the last generation for an Afro-centric curriculum, they often departed from the psychological model of white professional educators who wanted to promote social harmony by showing the "contributions" of all groups to a common society. Many African-American school reformers have used a political model instead. They have wanted a black-centered curriculum that could mobilize their people to change the circumstances of their lives by understanding how they had been victimized and by setting their own group goals. In 1954 W. E. B. Du Bois had thought that blacks might "eventually surrender race solidarity and the idea of American Negro culture to the concept of world humanity, above race and nation." The persistence of racism, however, continued to make this seem a distant as well as an ambiguous goal.[48]

School Policies on Gender

The civil rights movement provided one strategy of change to feminists in the 1960s and 1970s who attacked a pervasive sexism that limited females both in school and later in their adult lives. The term "sexism" was adapted from the word "racism," and both words designated forms of discrimination deeply embedded in institutions and in harmful social constructions of diversity.[49]

The social construction of gender and of race limited the life chances of white women and blacks (both female and male). Both groups were denied the vote and other rights of citizens. Initially, they were not allowed to attend any school, because white men declared that blacks and women lacked the brains to benefit from schooling. When blacks and white women did enter schools, their schooling was initially segregated and underfinanced. And because both white women and blacks were restricted to segmented labor markets and faced wage discrimination, their economic returns on schooling were far less than those of white males. In the middle of the twentieth century, white female and black male college graduates were paid about the same as white males who graduated only from elementary school. To be born female or black male, given the cultural construction of gender and race that shaped participation in key institutions, was thus to share some common disadvantages. To be born both black and female was potentially to face double forms of discrimination.[50]

Despite these parallels, gender operated differently from race in a number of ways in public schools. One striking contrast was the process of desegregation of the races versus the coeducation of the sexes. Horace Mann called the gradual evolution of coeducation "smuggling in the girls." The entry of girls into public schools took place quietly during the first half of the nineteenth century, with little debate, until by 1850 it was standard practice in most public schools. By contrast, racial desegregation was, and is, a highly contentious affair in most communities. It took a Civil War to open the doors of southern public schools to blacks, and those institutions remained almost all segregated by race until the late 1960s.[51]

Another point of difference between gender and race: Girls and boys have performed about the same academically in school whereas the races have not. Gender cuts across class and ethnic lines. Boys and girls shared the whole spectrum of white class and cultural backgrounds; they lived together on both sides of the railroad tracks and in homes that represented a cross section of cultural backgrounds. A disproportionate number of black families, by contrast, have been poor and attended meagerly supported schools, and that has handicapped their academic performance.[52]

Blacks *knew* that they were members of an oppressed group. When they sought to gain their educational rights as citizens, they had a strong sense of being a collectivity and could target specific forms of educational discrimination. Under the racial caste system whites kept down blacks by segregating them and starving their schools' resources.

White women, however, did not necessarily think that they had been treated unfairly in school. Few laws or explicit school policies treated the sexes differently. When educators did differentiate between boys and girls—often in informal or unconscious ways—many women and men saw nothing wrong since they accepted traditional gender roles as part of the natural order. So the few policies that treated girls and boys differently were typically not seen as discriminatory, at least until recent years.[53]

Public discourse about gender policies in schools has reflected conflicting views about how men and women should relate to each other. It still does. Worries about whether women were overstepping their proper sphere or whether men were insufficiently masculine have spilled over into arguments about gender in schools. At different times critics have said that the schools make the girls too masculine or the boys too feminine. Only rarely have activists claimed that schools made the girls too feminine and the boys too masculine, for educators have only rarely sought to alter gender stereotypes.[54]

There has been a strange relation between policy talk, silence, and gender practice in the schools. The biggest change in gender practice, the desegregation of the sexes, took place largely without serious controversy. Educators seemed to like coeducation for reasons of institutional convenience more than ideology. When critics of coeducation railed about the "boy problem" or the "woman issue," they had relatively small impact on what happened in schools.

For all the talk about gender policies, the basic institutional pattern of coeducation in public schools has remained remarkably stable for a century. Despite some minor curricular differentiation by sex, as in vocational education, girls and boys have mostly studied the same subjects together as if they were institutionally interchangeable. The same was hardly true of blacks and whites. Under the caste system they attended separate schools and often studied different subjects.

In the nineteenth century most advocates of coeducation assumed that girls had the capacity and the need to learn more or less what boys learned. The academic performance of girls—who consistently won higher grades than boys—proved their capacity, and their enthusiasm for schooling demonstrated their commitment to learning. Although activists in the woman's movement demanded that all spheres of activity be open to women, most nineteenth-century educators believed that women had a different destiny from that of men. They were to employ their schooling in the separate sphere of women: the family and suitably female services such as teaching. Thus pioneers in the education of women stressed both the similar mental abilities of boys and girls and the different social destinies of women and men. Indeed, girls entered coeducational classrooms at roughly the time when Victorian opinion-shapers were most eager to separate adult women into their own sphere.[55]

A long tradition of both garden-variety prejudice and "scientific" inquiry, however, maintained that women and men were essentially different in intellect and temperament as well as in social function. The doctrine of sex differences, therefore, was anathema to feminists who recognized this ideology as a prop of gender injustice, a way to keep women in their place. Early in the twentieth century a generation of talented women psychologists demolished one by one the propositions of a pseudo-science that justified a subordinate role for women by asserting that they were "different," usually meaning inferior. Most feminist pioneers argued that coeducation was appropriate because girls and boys were mentally equal.[56]

In the early 1970s feminist researchers who investigated gender practices in schools found that coeducational schools were not, in fact, egalitarian. They documented gender biases such as these in order to convince policymakers that there was a problem:

Textbooks either ignored females or portrayed them in highly traditional roles.

Counselors, responding "realistically" to the job market, steered girls to traditionally female occupations.

Studies of teachers' behavior claimed that there was systematic bias—teachers paid more attention to boys and challenged them intellectually more than girls.

Few women occupied positions of leadership in schools (such as superintendent or principal).

Sports, vocational education, and some other official activities of the schools were segregated by sex (and girls typically received fewer resources in their segregated activities).[57]

For the most part, such discrimination was largely unconscious, implicit rather than explicit, built into the school as *institutional sexism* that was often more difficult to attack than obvious and deliberate bias. What was necessary, thought many reformers, was to make coeducation truly identical, to eliminate differential treatment of girls and boys, men and women.

In the last three decades, however, some feminist scholars have challenged both the doctrine of similarity of the sexes and the prac-

tice of coeducation. They have argued that differences of cultural
experience (but not distinct genes) have produced qualities of character and intellect that distinguish women from men. These qualities, they claim, are not honored in male-dominated coeducational
schools that stress abstract thought over interrelatedness, assertive-
ness over compassion, and competition over cooperation. One lesson drawn from this position is that the differences in power and
character between men and women make coeducation a recipe for
continuing educational subordination.[58]

The arguments over sexual similarities and differences, like similar disputes about race, have shifted markedly over time and have
shaped proposals for school reform. The ideal of color-blind and
sex-neutral schools now makes little sense to people who believe
that such neutrality is impossible—that in fact such a school would
simply express the dominant outlooks of white males. A belief in
the basic similarity of boys and girls as learners undergirded coeducation, but a notion of crucial gender differences is now used to
argue for all-girl schools or for a new, "gender-sensitive" form of coeducation. "In a society in which traits are genderized and socialization according to sex is common," writes Jane Roland Martin,
"an educational philosophy that tries to ignore gender in the name
of equality is self-defeating." From this point of view, gender blindness could make the real problems invisible.[59]

Diversity and Unity

Underlying most policy discussion about social diversity in education are two contrasting points of view on sameness and difference.
One assumes that civic unity is possible because people are basically alike, no matter what groups they may belong to (a variant of
this approach holds that people may be initially quite different but

are capable of becoming the same if properly instructed). The other stresses basic differences between groups. Each perspective on sameness and difference contains germs of truth, but each also reveals serious flaws both in describing social reality and in prescribing social policy.

The common school reformers of the nineteenth century hoped that the right kind of education could render heterogeneous people alike. The same idea shaped the crusade to assimilate American Indians to "civilized" ways. It persisted in the campaign to Americanize the children of immigrants during the Progressive era. In the 1950s it undergirded the ideology of liberal educators who sought to be race blind, gender blind, and class blind. It inspired those in the 1960s who believed that compensatory instruction could overcome the handicaps imposed by poverty. And it underlay the faith of those integrationists who believed that blacks and whites differed chiefly in the color of their skins.

Educational leaders who believed in the potential similarity of all people shared an optimistic and generous faith yet sometimes suffered from tunnel vision. Confident in their own "mainstream" values, which they hoped all individuals could hold in common, they failed to understand the persistence and power of cultural and ethnic loyalties. They sometimes also underestimated the benefits that dominant groups gained from discrimination. Race continued to divide society. Gross economic inequalities persisted, and the poor remained at a severe disadvantage in school and society as income became more and more unequal.

People who believed that groups were basically different have varied in how they understood this human dissimilarity. Some used socially constructed concepts of difference to subordinate other people. Under the southern caste system, for example, whites defined blacks as a distinct and inferior group, segregated them, and exploited them. Blacks joined forces to resist such subordination, recognizing their common degradation and banding together to achieve liberation. In this case group identity worked to liberate blacks from racism. When they had won the legal right to attend schools with whites, however, some blacks decided that they preferred separate schools. With blacks in charge, their children could escape white racists, learn their own heritage, gain a sense of racial pride, and mobilize to achieve political and economic goals. "Race" in that sense was experienced as a positive common bond.

In the past, when educators talked about "intercultural education" or "pluralism," they generally believed that individuals of different ethnic groups would eventually become assimilated. Celebrating diverse cultures would make that process less divisive and painful. In recent years some advocates have gone beyond celebration of diversity and designed schools that would preserve group identities. Individuals, they believe, can best realize themselves through such group membership. The power of the public school system should be employed not to eradicate ethnic differences but to preserve and strengthen them.

People who stress group solidarity as a way to reform education offer a useful counterweight to the competitive individualism and cultural homogeneity that characterize many schools. They may exaggerate, however, the fixity of group boundaries and blur the great variety of opinion and condition within groups. Within ethnoracial groups, for example, members debate about the policies that should inform the education of their children. Mexican-Americans generally want their children to learn English because they want them to have access to opportunities in the larger society, but may not be of one mind about the role of the school in maintaining their ancestral language and culture. Blacks often disagree about desegregation.[60]

Is there solid footing to be found among these competing positions on ethnicity, race, and gender? What might be some principles to follow in creating cultural democracy? I think that my Cape Verdean friends Paul and Gus might have wanted Americans to be cautious about the relentless urge to classify and stratify, to assign people to their supposed places. Respect the ways people define themselves. Make sure that they have the common rights and opportunities that all citizens should enjoy. Teach them to care that others have those rights and opportunities as well.

CHAPTER FOUR

Thoroughly Trained in Failure: Mismatch of Pupil and School

HELEN Todd knew many children who had majored in failure in school. She was a child labor inspector in Chicago early in the twentieth century. Her work required her to go into the factories of the city where boys and girls stripped tobacco leaves, made paper boxes, lacquered canes, and ran endless errands. These were the kind of young people who today might be called "at risk." Despite the boredom of the repetitive work, long hours, and miserable working conditions, most of the young workers she talked with did not want to return to school.[1]

"School ain't no good," said one of Todd's child workers. "When you works a whole month at school, the teacher she gives you a card to take home that says how you ain't any good. And yer folks hollers on yer an' hits yer." Another told Todd: "You never understands what they tells you in school, and you can learn right off to do things in a factory." Over and over again the young workers told her that teachers beat them for not learning, or not standing up or sitting down on command, or forgetting the correct page in recitation.[2]

"Would it not be possible," Todd asked, "to adapt this child of foreign peasants less to education, and adapt education more to the

child? . . . Nothing that a factory sets them to do is so hard, so ter-
rifying, as learning. . . . We do not make our education fit their psychology, their traditions, their environment or inheritance." Todd
was ahead of her time in stressing the *school's* responsibility for the
mismatch between schools and students who did not fit the mainstream mold.[3]

In 1909 Todd asked 500 children between the ages of fourteen
and sixteen this question: "If your father had a good job and you
didn't have to go to work, which would you do—go to school or
work in a factory?" More than 80 percent said that they preferred
the factory over the school, the paycheck over the report card.
Todd's child laborers were hardly unique in their headlong rush to
keep out of classrooms. In the neighboring city of Milwaukee, reformers offered to pay youths 75 cents a day if they went to school
full time instead of attending continuation schools part time and
working the rest of the week in menial jobs. The 75 cents was
about what they would have received at work. Out of 8,000
youths offered this incentive to go to school, only 16 accepted.[4]

Todd was dealing with children who fled school. Many other
children and youth remained unschooled because they were denied entry to classrooms. As late as 1970, the federal census
counted about two million children between seven and seventeen
who were not enrolled in school. In a comprehensive survey, the
Children's Defense Fund found that the census underestimated the
actual number of absentees. Who were these young people? "We
found," the Fund said, "that if a child is not white, or is white but
not middle class, does not speak English, is poor, needs special help
with seeing, hearing, walking, reading, learning, adjusting, growing
up, is pregnant or married at age 15, is not smart enough or too
smart, then, in many places, school officials decide school is not the
place for that child."[5]

Todd's factory children and the young people excluded from

school illustrate extreme cases of misfit between schools and the children they were supposed to serve. In a less dramatic way, however, students who have struggled to learn, or resisted the teacher, or failed academically have long been part of the everyday world of teachers. Diversity of academic performance has always been a fact of life in classrooms. How to make sense of that diversity—how to explain and remedy the failure of some students to learn what the school tries to teach—is one of the most persistent questions teachers face. Coping with academic diversity has become more complicated as school attendance has become more universal.

Educators have usually accepted differences in academic performance as just the way things were—like Original Sin or leaky roofs. From time to time, however, reformers have come to believe that the educational system required not a tune-up but a major overhaul if the school was not to be a factory of failure for huge numbers of students. So great was the weight of hopes and fears that Americans placed on their public schools that the accusation of failure rapidly became a call for action.[6]

In those periods of renewed awareness of failure, different cohorts of educators have pinned hundreds of different labels on children who failed to perform as the school expected. Stanley Zehm wrote astutely about such labeling and collected a rich array of different names given to "laggards." Such labels are telling. They reveal much about how educators sought to explain and remedy failure in school. Today, for example, think of the quite different messages contained in terms such as *at risk, struggling, developmentally delayed,* or *school weary.*[7]

Labels varied in different times and social contexts, urban and rural. In the nineteenth century teachers typically used a moral calculus for failure in school: that boy is *wicked* and *lazy* and needs to be whipped. The problem of failure was usually least obvious in classrooms that were least systematic, such as the country one-room classrooms. As school systems came to be bureaucratized into distinct grades in the years from 1850 to 1900, institutional explanations found favor: that girl is *slow* and needs to be assigned to a slow-paced track. In the Progressive era, humanitarians thought that many children were failing in school because they were *underprivileged;* a remedy was to give them health and social services. Advocates of vocational education knew that the *hand-minded* boy needed shop work, not more academic classes. By the 1920s experts on testing thought the cause of failure was obvious and suggested a remedy: *students of low IQ* lacked academic ability and should be sequestered in special classes. Many curriculum designers thought that the old one-size-fits-all program of studies led to failure; the cure was differentiation in the school program, a proper niche for every child. And so it went, as different educators in different times diagnosed different failures and prescribed different remedies. Failure was a rich vein for speculation.[8]

Foot Lads in Rural Schools

Common school advocates during the mid-nineteenth century believed that the school should train the rising generation in morality, citizenship, and the basic skills represented by the Three Rs. Crusaders for public education agreed that ideally the rich and the poor should have basically the same education. "Our main object is to secure the benefits of education for those who would otherwise be destitute," said workingmen in Philadelphia, "and to place them mentally on a level with the most favored in the world's gifts." The public school should make real "the glorious principle and vivifying declaration that 'all men are created equal.'"[9]

Common school activists shared an underlying conviction that even a rudimentary educational system—one that theoretically mixed together all the children of all the people in a free and public institution—could preserve the republic and provide a basic equality of educational opportunity. Even a brief exposure to the common school should prepare students to compete on equal terms in adult life. If children had this similar opportunity, then it was primarily the fault of individual pupils if they did not succeed in school and life.[10]

Since the United States was primarily a rural nation—about 70 percent of students attended rural schools as late as 1890—the major agency of public education was the one-room schools in dispersed agricultural communities. Children attended class only a few months a year; formal schooling was only a casual and occasional part of their lives. Alvin Johnson remembered that when he had been a student in rural Maine in the 1880s "my early schooling interfered very little with my education. We expected to learn nothing in school, and were not disappointed." Often the one-room school became a battleground of wills between the male teachers and the older male students, a contest in which each sought to humiliate the other.[11]

The child who acted up or did not learn what the teacher taught might be caned, in part because of an assumption that the reluctant learner lacked character. When teachers of the early nineteenth century described poor performers (usually male), they used words like *dunce, shirker, loafer, idle, vicious, reprobate, depraved, wayward, wrong-doer, sluggish, scapegrace, stupid,* and *incorrigible.* Although terms such as *dunce* and *stupid* suggest that educators sometimes saw low achievement as the result of lack of smarts, far more often they thought that the child who did not do well in school was deficient in virtue. That was serious because the chief purpose of the common school was to educate citizens of sound character.[12]

Underlying the labels was a religious and moral world-view: Individuals were responsible for learning and good behavior. There was competition in rural classrooms, as in spelling bees, in which good students could vie to go to the head of the class. The bad boys who fell to the foot of the class were called foot lads. These incipient ruffians could prove their cleverness and bad morals to their peers by refusing to be humiliated by their failure, as Warren Burton reminisced: "Let it not be thought that these foot lads are deficient in intellect. Look at them when the master's back is turned, and you will see mischievous ingenuity enough to convince you that they surpass even James and Harriet, the best spellers in the class, had some other faculties been called into exercise beside the mere memory of verbalities."[13] Though mischief had its rewards in the form of admiration from the peer group, in the immensely popular *McGuffey Readers* virtue always triumphed.

A rural boy or girl who did not do well in school had many other ways of demonstrating competence and achieving recognition. There was plenty of work to do on the farm and in the home, and young people could demonstrate skills in hunting or embroidery that would impress family and friends. And in the nongraded, informal structure of the rural school pupils could progress informally at their own pace, making "failure" more obscure.[14]

Factories of Failure

By contrast, failing and passing were defining features of bureaucratized urban education. "Laggards," or children held back in grade because they failed the exams for promotion, became the familiar product of a rigid system that sought to process large batches of children in uniform ways. This outcome was ironic, for equality and efficiency were prime goals of the urban graded school. The architects of urban education were confident that by making schools systematic and uniform they were rendering them more failure proof. They wanted to avoid the haphazard and diverse character of rural schools. The graded school, a standardized curriculum chopped up into desiccated chunks, and annual testing programs to determine promotion to the next grade—these were premised on the notion that children could and should be taught the same subjects, in the same way, and at the same pace. It was obvious that flunking a grade was painful, but Walt Whitman complained that creative children also suffered agonies in such a mechanical system: "*stupid dull boy.* Such is the name frequently applied to youths who are really profound, and have souls too swelling for the monotonous bounds of rule and rote."[15]

The urban graded school separated children into supposedly uniform groups by academic proficiency (which mostly corresponded with age). Gradation of classes became popular in large part because it promised the efficiency of the division of labor common in factories. Eager to align the elements of the school system, educators arranged the curriculum into standardized parts that corresponded with the grades, year by year. Urban normal schools trained teachers in the specific curriculum and pedagogy approved by the district. At the end of the year pupils took a test to demonstrate that they had learned the studies for that grade and were ready to move to the next level. Success meant moving up the ladder. Failure meant staying in place or being condemned to the "ungraded" classroom where truants, cut-ups, and "backward" children gathered. Urban school leaders such as William T. Harris were forever tinkering with the system of gradation and promotion, recognizing that even in the best systems there were "leftover" children.[16]

At the top of the nineteenth-century arch of urban schooling was the meritocratic and graded high school. Tests to enter the high school were often very difficult, and flunking rates high. Far from defining failures in these examinations as a problem, many educators saw them instead as a sign that academic standards were being maintained and diligent students properly rewarded.[17]

In many cities there were not nearly enough seats in elementary school for all the children legally entitled to an education. In 1886 Chicago had room for only one third of its school-age cohort, and in Buffalo in 1873 about half the children would have found no seats. In this economy of educational scarcity—only slowly remedied—few people worried much about the losers, those young people who hated the classroom, or did not find a place in school, or who were pushed out by the system.[18]

How did urban educators of the latter half of the nineteenth century label students who did not keep up with the factory-like pace of the elementary grades and the meritocratic competition of secondary schooling? Some of the epithets suggested the earlier view that academic failure came from bad character or faulty dispositions: *weak, uncouth, stubborn*. If pupils did not learn, it was largely their own fault. From her rich sample of accounts of nineteenth-century classrooms Barbara Jean Finkelstein concluded that teachers believed that "the acquisition of knowledge represented a triumph of the will as well as the intellect. Consistently, . . . teachers treated academic failure, not as evidence of their own inabilities as instructors, but as evidence of the students' personal and moral recalcitrance." Increasingly as the century moved on, educators came to associate the character defects of the pupils with the moral and social inadequacies of their families, especially in the case of immigrants.[19]

But some of the terms that educators used to describe poor performers—*leftover, dull, slow, immature, born-late, overgrown*—revealed an emerging institutional category of the "normal" student that turned the "slow" student into a deviant. The normal student was the one who proceeded at the regular pace demanded by the logic of a graded school—the batch-processing of pupils by the school bureaucracy. The student who flunked the promotion exam was held back and considered to be "retarded," or "laggard," a failure.

The superintendent of the Cincinnati public schools from 1874 to 1886, John Peaslee, worried about preoccupation with test results. Fear of failure and pressure to succeed were hurting both students and teachers. He told his teachers that reputations and jobs "would not depend upon the high percents . . . pupils might obtain in examinations, but on attention to duty, manners, mode of discipline, methods of instruction, and upon the tone of [the] school." It had been a mistake, he said, to put so much stress on test results: "In order to stimulate the teachers to greater expectations, the percents were posted up in the offices of the superintendents, . . . carried about in triumph by principals, paraded in the daily papers, and published in school reports. But it was found that attaching undue importance to percents leads to the driving and cramming process, to teaching in narrow ruts . . . [and] to drive poor pupils out of school."[20] To critics of high-stakes exams today these complaints may sound familiar.

In Cleveland in 1892 the superintendent decided to abolish promotional exams entirely, relying instead on the judgment of the teachers about whether the pupil was ready to go on to the next grade. This change, he said, was "an unqualified success. It has relieved the Superintendent's office, teachers, pupils, and parents of a strain upon time, energy and nerve power, and has produced very desirable pedagogic results." The next task was to reach the "leftover children," the nonpromoted students who were the ones needing "the most help and the best help, but in spite of all that is said and done . . . are liable to become discouraged . . . and frequently remain in the same grade two or three or even more years."[21]

Ending Failure?

The turn of the twentieth century was a time of intense attention to the defects of public education, when an epic struggle between the old education and the new was at hand. Much of what has been called "progressive education" was a campaign to reduce, or even eliminate, failure in schooling. A leader in this crusade was Leonard Ayres, who published in 1909 a book called *Laggards in the Schools.* "Thoroughly trained in failure" was the way he described children who were forced to repeat grades. Studies of "retardation" showed that a very large minority of students—estimated at one third—were denied promotion at least once.[22]

The result was that the vast majority of pupils were lumped in the lower grades of the system. In Tennessee in 1906 about 150,000 entered the first grade, 10,000 the eighth, and only 575 graduated from high school. Nationwide the comparable figures in city schools were 1,000, 263, and 56 in the high school senior class. In Memphis, Tennessee, 75 percent of black students were held back.[23]

There were too many "leftover children." The uniform graded school may have been efficient for the majority of students who matched its regime. But for vast numbers—especially impoverished immigrants and blacks—the system was geared to produce failure. To eliminate failure, many progressive reformers thought, it was time to build a new system, not simply fine-tune the old. They developed a new analysis and prescription of what equality of opportunity and democracy might mean in education: not the same curriculum for all but a different one for each. Do not expect all children to learn the same knowledge or skills, for their "configurations of mind" are different. In a properly designed school system there would be no failure (or at least it would be better disguised than in the older system of sink-or-swim exams for promotion).[24]

At that time reformers were most concerned about immigrant children, large numbers of whom clustered in the lower grades because they failed the annual examinations for promotion from grade to grade. These "laggards" of that era typically dropped out of school at an early age to enter dead-end jobs or joined the large bands of truants. In addition to immigrants, progressive reformers also worried about physically and mentally disabled children, those in impoverished rural schools, and boys (who had lower grades and higher dropout rates than girls). Early in this century relatively few white educators expressed concern, however, about the group that was clearly the most educationally underserved segment of the American population: African-Americans, who were afforded only a starvation diet of schooling in the caste system of the South and who were typically discriminated against in the North as well.[25]

Social and Health Services

When educational leaders and humanitarian reformers of the Progressive era became concerned about the legions of students who were held back in grades and who fled school as early as possible, they concluded that schools should greatly expand their functions. The pupils' problems were not just pedagogical. If children came to school hungry, or had toothaches, or couldn't see the numbers on the blackboard, or lacked money for school books and clothes, they were already on the road to failure. Reformers called for school-based health and social services in order to prevent or remedy poor academic achievement, ill-health, crime, child neglect, poverty, dropping out, addiction, hunger, pain, and unemployment.[26]

Reformers pressed for a whole array of child services—school lunches, medical and dental inspections and clinics, classes for handicapped and sick children, vocational guidance and placement, school social workers to counsel wayward youths and to assist their parents, summer schools to provide recreation and learning for urban children in the long hot summers, and child welfare officers to deal with truant and delinquent students. Some reformers created schools that were social centers, institutions that provided services for all members of immigrant families in their neighborhoods. In the 1930s Leonard Covello founded a noted community-centered high school in East Harlem. He regarded "failure at any age . . . [as] something the seriousness of which cannot be exaggerated. Forcing a boy who is an academic failure, or even a behavior problem, out of school solves nothing at all. The solution must be found within the school itself and the stigma of failure must be placed in a boy as seldom as possible."[27]

Initially, the impetus for health and social services in education came mostly from outside the schools. Public health doctors, local, state, and national medical groups, and dentists interested in preventive medicine were the pioneers in providing free inspections and clinics. Women's clubs took the initiative in many reforms, including free or cheap school meals, transportation and special classes for sickly or handicapped children, playgrounds, and vacation schools. In many cities, park and recreation programs collaborated with school districts in planning sites and sharing facilities. Settlement house workers pioneered in programs of school social work. Foundations and the federal government publicized and sometimes financed the new health and social services.[28]

The crusaders for these different services generally agreed that their programs would prevent or diminish failure in school. "Medical inspection became one of the most highly touted panaceas of the Progressive era," William J. Reese observes. "It was variously endorsed as a way to eliminate 'backward' and 'dull' students, to ensure all children equal educational opportunities, to promote the vitality of the 'race,' and to make parents more responsible citizens." Like doctors, dentists regarded their work as a cure-all, claiming that eliminating tooth decay would bring good health, lessen school failures, and even prevent delinquency. But whatever the hype about medical panaceas, the health problems of the immigrants were real enough. Diseases and physical defects, many of them readily correctible (such as near-sightedness), were rampant in poor and crowded urban ghettos.[29]

Nonprofessional voluntary groups were often responsible for the adoption of reforms in social services. Women's clubs, sometimes allied with elite groups such as New York's Public Education Association and sometimes with socialist leaders, pioneered in such reforms as free or cheap breakfasts or lunches, vacation schools, and playgrounds and other recreational facilities for the out-of-school hours. Reformers from settlement houses in urban slums pioneered new forms of school-linked social work and counseling. Social settlements were a model, also, for reformers who tried to make schools into community-based social centers.[30]

Drawing on their own experiences as mothers and (in many cases) as former teachers, women reformers had first-hand knowledge of the needs of children and the time and social connections helpful in bringing reforms to fruition. Proper nutrition for impoverished students was a common concern of those "domestic feminists" who sought to expand their scope as "municipal housekeepers" beyond the home. Scholarly studies confirmed the commonsense notion that a hungry child found it difficult to learn, and teachers agreed with the claims of the nutrition reformers that hungry scholars who were "restless, dull, and difficult to manage" became "studious, tractable, and bright" students when properly fed. Women's clubs provided free meals to poor children in dozens of cities but wanted school boards to install them "in all public schools as part of their work and not as a charity."[31]

Philanthropic women also created "vacation schools" for children who had no safe place to play and little adult supervision during sweltering summer days. They negotiated with urban school boards for free use of empty schools and paid the teachers from their own pockets. But these summer schools were more than supervised play; reformers used them to explore how to make schools more welcoming to children, not places of fear and failure. Advocates of vacation schools wanted them to be "pedagogic experiment stations" where progressive teaching methods had free rein. As they did in settlement house programs, children in summer schools took field trips to parks and to the countryside, studied nature, learned crafts, staged plays, and visited museums and other city attractions. This form of extended day care for children proved immensely popular with parents and pupils; demand far exceeded supply.[32]

Reformers in settlement houses pioneered another form of social service: visiting teachers (the forerunners of school social workers). In the beginning, the visiting teachers, volunteers or people paid by charitable contributions, served as bridges between immigrant homes and the schools. They visited classrooms and families to determine why children were truant or having difficulty in school. Although they sometimes pursued individual psychological case work with children, they more often served as social ombudspersons who sought to help immigrants adjust to a new land, to help educators interpret the mismatch between their pupils and the school, and to find needed resources for families and children.[33]

Unlike Covello, who continually adapted school services according to the advice of community residents, elite reformers generally thought that they knew what was best for immigrants and seldom asked their clients' opinions about new social and health programs. Many of the reformers used a deficit model in characterizing the people they sought to help, assuming that immigrants did not know about proper health and dental care, or nutrition, or acceptable civic values, or how to raise children, or even how to cook. The reformers had a millennial faith that their services could fix people: Clean mouths would produce clean minds; proper playgrounds would eliminate juvenile delinquency; removing adenoids would prevent academic failures; and vocational counselors could match youth with jobs through a smooth process of social engineering.[34]

Their clients were often on better speaking terms with reality. Immigrant parents found some programs helpful if not cure-alls. They were eager to place their children in the supervised vacation schools or to use school facilities for evening adult classes in sewing or English. Families struggling to make ends meet probably welcomed free or cheap breakfasts and lunches in the schools. Some women who sponsored these meals for children recognized that they had different tastes (thick soups for Italians, thin for the Irish, in one community school). Visiting teachers often were able to counsel parents and children and help them adjust to a strange new country.

But many immigrant parents fought the more intrusive and culturally insensitive activities of those who would improve them and their children. Fiercest was their reaction to medical interventions.

In New York in 1906 Jewish parents rioted outside a school when a rumor spread that the school officials were slitting the throats of their children; without parents' permission, doctors were excising the enlarged adenoids of students. "During the same year," Reese reports, "1,500 angry Italian mothers in Brooklyn fought police, pelted the local school with stones and other objects, and prevented any medical treatments." A mother complained to a teacher when she received a note from a medical inspector saying that her son smelled bad: "Teacher, Johnny ain't no rose. Learn him; don't smell him."[35]

People had mixed reactions to the new social services. Economy-minded school boards, struggling to provide enough seats in conventional classrooms for waves of incoming students, worried about who would pay for nonacademic services. Academic conservatives who wanted to stress traditional subjects sometimes saw the new services as a diversion from their central tasks. By contrast, progressive educators argued that compulsory attendance and child labor laws were bringing in new types of students and making it essential to broaden the scope of the school to include functions previously performed by family, workplace, church, and neighborhood. Students from impoverished families needed assistance to be able to succeed in school, and progressives sometimes envisaged the school itself as a service station. Over time some of the services became incorporated in school bureaucracies as programs of special education, health education, child services (the euphemistic label sometimes used to describe the activities of truant officers), counseling, and physical education and recreation.[36]

Health and social services were not the panaceas that their advocates sometimes claimed. But the reformers who wanted to give poor students a better start were at least aware of the misery of failing in school and eager to equalize opportunity. These services made it possible for many needy students to cope with school. But educational leaders of the Progressive era had plans that were far more ambitious than providing services. They were ready to redefine opportunity and democracy.

Differentiation and Democracy

Early in the twentieth century, many educational leaders sought a new blueprint for equality and democracy in public schools. The old system of expecting all students to master the same academic curriculum they dismissed as rigid and cruel. It was, they thought, a Procrustean bed on which the wits of the bright were cramped and the talents of the dull unduly stretched. One size did not fit all in education, and equality did not mean sameness. Democracy in education should provide equality and diversity of opportunity, the chance to rise as far as one's abilities permitted.[37]

The progressives' logic was simple enough. People are different in academic abilities (the IQ test allegedly showed that) talents, interests, tastes, inclinations, career goals, dispositions, and home backgrounds. Why shouldn't the curriculum reflect those differences? Why shouldn't students have a choice of what they studied?

Many citizens thought that they, too, should have a say about what those students learned. It wasn't just educators who wanted to expand the course of studies. Beginning in the nineteenth century, and increasingly in the twentieth, dozens of interest groups stood ready to cure civic ills or help business by yet adding another course to the curriculum (often on a subject remote from the traditional academic disciplines). The National Association of Manufacturers supported vocational education as a cure for the supposed incompetence or indiscipline of American workers (compared with Germans, for example). The Women's Christian Temperance Union lobbied states and the federal government until they legislated an anti-alcohol message in every school in the nation. A preferred cure for carnage on the highway was driver education, cheerfully advocated by car dealers and insurance companies. Students initiated high school varsity sports programs, those icons of the complete secondary school. State legislators enacted laws requiring compulsory physical education after huge numbers of draftees failed their physical exams. When public health officials battled an epidemic of venereal disease around 1900, they proposed classes in sex education. The American Legion and the Daughters of the American Revolution lobbied tirelessly to Americanize America through instruction in patriotism.[38]

Every other group in town or in the state capitols, it seemed, wanted to exercise its democratic prerogatives by proposing some new course. Curriculum theorists sometimes complained about the way lay interest groups were invading what should be a professional domain, curriculum construction. A major challenge for educational leaders was to invent or create some coherence in the many piecemeal programs added to the curriculum by lay groups as well as by professional educators. At times it seemed that nothing was too trivial for pupils to study if it enhanced "life adjustment." If students did not visibly fail in such courses, it's questionable that they learned much, either.[39]

In the nineteenth century, educators typically justified academic subjects by appealing to tradition and by claiming that they trained the mind. Progressive educators said they trained for "life," but the incoherence of the add-on curriculum led reformers in the 1970s to compare high schools with shopping malls, institutions that were united by common heating systems and parking lots, but not by a common mission other than attracting customers. The issue of diversity and choice in curriculum is one to which I will return in Chapter 6.[40]

Most progressive educators and school boards and local citizens were unabashedly proud of the large new high schools that offered a broad array of programs. Educational leaders lamented that thousands of small high schools could afford only a spare, usually traditional academic, course of study. Differentiation represented *progress*, and burgeoning enrollments seemed to prove the value of responding to the diversity of students by expanding the course of study and elaborating the structures of schooling.

Vocational education became the flagship of curricular differentiation, supported by an implausibly broad band of advocates: the National Association of Manufacturers, the U.S. Chamber of Commerce, the American Federation of Labor, noted humanitarians, and the energetic educators of the National Society for the Promotion of Industrial Education. Such lobbies claimed that vocational education would help the United States compete with other countries, reduce industrial conflict, and increase the productivity and pay of workers. There is little evidence that vocational education succeeded in meeting such extrinsic goals, but many vocational courses appealed to pupils alienated by their experiences in traditional graded classrooms. In shop and home economics students learned skills and knowledge different from those in academic courses. Many students found the shop or kitchen a more engaging environment than the traditional classroom, for there they had a chance to move about, produce a product, talk while working on cooperative tasks, and learn skills that they could promptly use.[41]

It was an article of progressive faith that every student should be able to succeed at something. In 1923 a California educator pointed out that students who had flunked grades in elementary or junior high school were entering high schools. These pupils, she believed, lacked the ability to succeed in traditional high school courses. All youths, she said, had in common certain "aspirations and responsibilities," such as becoming economically independent and being well regarded by peers, and desiring to "produce or create something." But not all students could learn standard academic subjects, and as a result, "too often the only thing the limited pupil gets from the high school is a sense of failure." When there was a mismatch between the traditional school and the new pupils, the modern solution was to offer variety and choice. Teachers and counselors should "find at least one worth-while thing at which the limited child can succeed, train him in this, and let him feel honest success." That was the democratic way, she thought, and that was the humane way.[42]

Urban school leaders in the 1920s and 1930s tried a variety of strategies to fit schooling to the "new" students flocking into the upper grades of the elementary schools and into the high schools. The Denver public schools, for example, created a number of separate schools for immigrant children who did not know English, for children who fell behind because they were sick, for the gifted, and for disabled, blind, or deaf children. They created special classes for children forced to repeat grades, and they divided elementary schools into classes that proceeded at different paces. They differentiated the curriculum in large high schools into tracks and added a host of new courses, many of them vocational. And they created elaborate testing and counseling systems designed to sort students into tracks and niches and to help them select courses. They believed that this elaboration of choices to fit the span of human abilities and aspirations was the new Jerusalem of democracy, a realistic form of equality of opportunity.[43]

Determinism with a Smiling Face

Even before the development of group intelligence testing during World War I, some educators and lay people were beginning to conclude that a substantial proportion of students were incapable of mastering the standard academic curriculum. As early as 1898 the superintendent of the Baltimore public schools was dividing students into three groups (normal, below, above) on the basis of their "mental capacities" and their "future possibilities." He developed a separate set of requirements for each group. When IQ tests were employed in schools in massive numbers during the 1920s, they seemed to confirm the garden-variety prejudice that there were not only incapable individuals but incapable groups (though testers admitted that there might be talented persons even in what they considered to be the most unpromising ethnic or class groupings).[44]

The labels educators used during the period from 1900 to 1950 indicate a significant shift from the nineteenth century in the way they thought about the "misfits" in the educational system: *pupils of low IQ, low-division pupils, ne'er-do-wells, sub-z group, limited, slow learners, laggards, vocational, backward, occupational, mental deviates,* and (bluntly) *inferior.* The message of the labels was clear: There were students who simply did not have smarts. The scientific solution was to teach them different things in a different way, and perhaps in a different place, from the "normal" students.[45]

In theory, the new differentiated curriculum gave rich opportunities to students to choose programs or courses. In practice, it is hard to tell how much students actually chose their programs and how much they were steered into different programs by educators. The new "scientific" experts had a deep faith in the wisdom of using tests to slot students into different courses and curriculums and occupations. Thanks to this "science of human nature," E. L. Thorndike said in 1913, "the average graduate of Teachers College in 1950 ought to be able to give better advice to a high school boy about the choice of an occupation than Solomon, Socrates, and

Benjamin Franklin all together could give." Such leaders had a vision of a smoothly engineered school and society in which failure was a thing of the past, not because all children were born equal in abilities but because educational science could find a place for all children, whatever their abilities, and steer them to that place.[46]

As genetic determinism began to creep into the discourse of educators, they did not abandon the language of "democracy." David Corson, the superintendent of schools in Newark, New Jersey, claimed in 1920 that the schools must provide new kinds of "equal opportunity" to children who were (presumably) genetically inferior:

> All children are not born with the same endowments or possibilities; they cannot be made equal in gifts or development or efficiency. The ultimate barriers are set by a power inexorable. There are in the schools tens of thousands of children over age physiologically, but only five, six, or seven years old mentally. The educational system must therefore be adjusted to meet this condition, so that the democratic theory of "equal opportunity" for all may be fully exemplified as well as preached.[47]

The democratic educator must face facts, he said. Because of unequal genetic inheritances, equal education cannot mean the same education.

The superintendent realized that he was treading on thin ice in talking this way about IQ, however. He warned teachers against using labels such as "slow" in public, for "it is insidious and undemocratic to call a child *slow* or to classify him at all in ordinary conversation or practice." Let's keep that our professional secret as we attend to our public relations. In Corson's view it was democratic to diversify the curriculum but undemocratic to talk to the public about tracking. Determinism, yes, but with a smiling face.

Detroit offers an illustration of how one large district tried to fit schooling and vocation to the "configurations of mind" of its different students. The supposed three major categories of intellect—abstract, abstract-motor, and motor—were mirrored in the types of school programs and in the college or vocational destinations open to the three kinds of students. In such a deterministic hierarchy as this there were in theory no misfits. If school officials categorized you as "motor," you were expected to end up pushing a broom or working on the assembly line at Ford; if you scored high on "abstract," you should go on to higher education and a profession. Pride of place and career rewards went to those who took academic courses in the college track.[48]

The Detroit plan to channel students is a striking example of educators engaged in social engineering. It shows how some educators hoped to eliminate failure in schools by perfectly aligning the abilities and destinies of pupils, educational programs, and jobs.

I've suggested that the educators who sought to redesign education were dealing with real problems: Students and schools were seriously mismatched; legions of children were failing to meet the demands they faced in school. But the redesign of the curriculum, including the vocational tracks, also created the rigidity of a deterministic world in which supposed mental capacity predetermined opportunity.

Social Protest, Labels, and School Failure

Many people, both inside and outside schools, disagreed with the use of IQ tests and labels to divide and differentiate. Critics said that this concept of diversity was infected with class bias and ethnic discrimination. In a report published in 1924 the Chicago Federation of Labor dissented vigorously from the use of IQ tests to track children in school and into occupations. Tracking students was not democratic but autocratic. "Has a new natural law been discovered," asked the Federation, "which binds each individual to a place in society and against which struggle is useless?" Determinism with a smile was still determinism.[49]

For most of the twentieth century, educators themselves had taken the initiative in devising solutions to the mismatch of student and school. But beginning in the late 1950s, a new set of actors entered school politics. They sought to redefine both the central educational problems and the solutions. Starting with blacks in the civil rights movement and spreading to other groups—Hispanics, women, advocates for the handicapped, native Americans, and others—outsiders who had been ignored or underserved demanded new influence over education.[50]

Members of these social movements typically rejected earlier labels for their children. They disagreed with diagnoses that blamed the parents for cultural "deficits" or located the trouble in the defects of individual students (whether faulty character or chromosomes). Instead, they uncovered examples of institutional racism and sexism. They demanded equality of access, as in integration of black and white schools, or opening sports or vocational programs to girls, or the mainstreaming of children with disabilities. They supported demands for equal resources and compensation for past inequities. They lobbied for bilingual programs for children of immigrants. They recommended broadening the curriculum to honor the cultural diversity of the society. The targets of these protest groups were both the obvious and the hidden injuries of race, gender, class, and cultural difference. The protesters wanted to adapt the school better to the child and called for a halt to blaming the victim.[51]

Some of the new names reformers gave to children who were not performing well in school began to reflect new ways of seeing.

Such terms as these, emerging in the period from 1950 to 1980, suggested that the blame lay more with the school than with the students: *the rejected, educationally handicapped, forgotten children, educationally deprived, culturally different,* and *pushouts.* But the older habits of thought remained embedded in labels like these: *socially maladjusted, terminal students, educationally difficult, marginal children, immature learners,* and *unwilling learners.* Such language still located the cause of the trouble largely in the student. In the public eye educators turned to euphemisms like *bluebirds* and *robins* to designate fast and slow reading groups.[52]

When educators responded to the demands of protest groups for greater social justice in education, they sometimes based their actions on old diagnoses. Some districts developed "compensatory" programs of remedial help. They believed this was a way to adapt schools better to "different" children. In practice, though, such programs often segregated and labeled children, just as Progressives had differentiated instruction for "misfits." Much of early compensatory education was based on a concept of deprivation and cultural deficit that betrayed a thin understanding of cultural differences. The "science" of education turned out to be not so objective, after all.[53]

Activists in protest movements and educational reformers were not satisfied with warmed-over solutions that carried new labels. They questioned the use of intelligence tests and the practice of tracking. They illuminated class and ethnic bias in the curriculum. They asked why it was that groups like blacks and Mexican-Americans were so overrepresented in classes for the mentally retarded. They called for attention to linguistic and cultural differences and promoted bilingual and multicultural education. In raising such issues they were rejecting labels that had ignored or demeaned or sequestered their children.[54]

No Child Left Behind?

Today, policymakers in education have once again rediscovered failure and are calling for nothing less than a failure-free educational system. The name of the act passed in 2001 by both parties in Congress and signed by President Bush tells its aim: No Child Left Behind. Whereas the Progressives fought failure by proposing different studies for different students, reformers in recent years want all students to reach proficiency in the same academic fields, especially reading and mathematics. The new federal act declares that achievement gaps between different groups of students must close. Under its provisions, school districts and states have a dozen years to raise all groups—rich and poor, brown, black, and white— to proficiency in mathematics and reading.[55]

Federal and state governments are immersing themselves in the nitty-gritty and jargon of school reform. Politicians talk about disaggregating test scores to compare the progress of different economic classes and ethnic groups. They debate the virtues of criterion-referenced testing (aligned with the curriculum) versus norm-referenced tests (designed to compare students). They condemn social promotion and call for high-stakes exams for passing students from one grade to the next and for graduation from high school. Reformers demand evidence that schools are teaching and children learning. And they insist on accountability, another name for whom to blame if things go wrong. Time to tighten up, they say. Set high standards, stress traditional subjects, give educators and students incentives for achievement and penalties for failure, and produce equality of results, no child left behind.[56]

This current campaign to assure academic success for all is new in scale if not in rhetoric. *Business Week* called it "wildly ambitious" in aim, nothing less than "declaring that in the Information Age, a solid education is a fundamental civil right." But attacking failure in education has a long history. Often the solutions of one period have led to still other kinds of failure or inequality. How to educate those who need good education the most, and who often perform least well in school, has challenged every generation, though in different ways and with varying intensity.[57]

Some students have always failed to learn what the school tried to teach them. Such failures were less obvious and consequential in some settings than in others. In the rural one-room school of the nineteenth century students dropped in and out of school and learned more or less at their own pace. Urban educators of that time, by contrast, built a graded system of instruction in which academic standards were clear and challenging, instruction was uniform, and flunking promotional exams was all too common. Progressive educators of the twentieth century argued that their predecessors had created factories of failure, systems of instruction that were cruel and inefficient. These twentieth-century reformers had their own "democratic" solution: Do not expect all students to learn the same things. Instead, differentiate the course of study and help each student find a niche where she or he can be successful.

Reformers' arguments about academic achievement and failure often have revolved around these questions: Are students basically similar or different? Should they follow the same course of study and be held to the same standard of proficiency? At one extreme were some leaders in nineteenth-century urban schools who seemed to treat pupils as malleable and the curriculum as a constant, while on the other extreme in the Progressive era some theorists seemed to regard the pupil as a constant (shaped by genes) and the curriculum as malleable if not infinitely expandable.

At the turn of the twenty-first century the advocates of sameness in curriculum hold front stage center. Most policy talk and action favors a uniform system of instruction. "Decide what every child should know and be able to do" is a mantra of the standards movement. In theory, standardized tests hold students and teachers accountable for following a prescribed curriculum.

The No Child Left Behind Act builds on two decades of attempts to raise academic standards. Because it is designed to bring all students up to a common standard, it pays close attention to groups of children who often have been undereducated. It mandates that states break out test scores by "poverty, race, ethnicity, disability, and limited English proficiency to ensure that no group is left behind." If all this works according to plan, the achievement gaps should narrow, and there should be fewer systematic failures.[58]

If all goes according to plan—there's the rub, for in the past, attacks on failure have often had unexpected and undesirable spin-offs and spill-overs. In its own way this contemporary vision is as utopian as any prior attack on school failure.

Creating standards itself is a daunting task. Some find new history standards unpatriotic; others find them insufficiently multicultural. The field of English seems in perpetual deconstruction. The New Math wars with the Old Math.

Developing tests that adequately assess what pupils have learned is a costly, difficult, and time-consuming task, and teaching students to do well on a poor test is a waste of time. For the students, taking rigorous tests on subjects that were never taught to them, or were unskillfully taught, is worse than a waste of time, for it undermines the students' self-confidence and makes a mockery of accountability.[59]

Some of the early results of high-stakes tests in this era of "no social promotion" are daunting. In 2001, 77 percent of students in New York City did not meet state standards of proficiency in eighth-grade mathematics, and 70 percent failed in reading. Abigail Thernstrom, a member of the Massachusetts State Board of Education, said it was a "ludicrous goal" to think that 100 percent of students could score at the "proficient" level. "At the moment," she said, "we in Massachusetts are just hoping that a respectable percentage of our kids manage to get into a low expectations, minimum skills category called 'Needs Improvement.' Those who do will get a high school diploma."[60]

Even if citizens and educators could agree on what every student should know, standards and high-stakes tests for promotion are unfair and futile if teachers and students do not have a chance to learn the prescribed subjects. That may seem obvious, yet all too many schools serving needy children lack staff trained to teach, for instance, algebra and geometry. Such schools need the most accomplished teachers, the smallest classes, buildings to be proud of, advanced academic courses as well as remedial ones, social and health services, stimulating after-school programs, and a rich curriculum that respects the cultures and taps the multiple talents of students.

Yet how often do schools with large concentrations of low-income and minority students have such resources? A few special schools do, and they have begun to close the achievement gaps. They should be encouraged and emulated. But so long as school resources continue to reflect the gross inequalities of wealth and income in this country, major achievement gaps will persist between the prosperous and the poor, and too many students will continue to be, now as in the past, "thoroughly trained in failure."

PART THREE

DEMOCRACY

Democracy in Education:
Who Needs It?

I N 1841 Darwin Atwater was school trustee and clerk of the common school in Mantua Village, Ohio. He waxed philosophical as he pondered the meaning of the new school term. "The earth in its annual revolution," he wrote in the trustees' minutes, prompts us to consider again "what has been done during the year that has past and what can be done during the year to come in the school in our neighborhood to forward the great enterprise of educating the human race." No task was more important than "to devise means to forward the education of our children who are soon to succeed us in active life and be our representatives for ages to come." Carrying out that mission, however, required more than lofty purpose. School boards also needed to levy local school taxes, to fix leaky roofs, to hire teachers each term, and to make sure that the citizens cut firewood small enough to fit into the school's stove. Two years later Atwater himself taught the school for forty-three days for a salary of fourteen dollars per month.[1]

In Mantua Village this mixture of the mundane and the eternal, the local and the cosmopolitan captured the work of rural school trustees as the common school movement spread across the nation. They were expected not only to see to the everyday details of running the local school district but also to mobilize collective choices, to help neighbors negotiate a sense of the common good. In these deliberations the invisible hand of republican ideology was often a more powerful force in shaping the common schools than the visible arm of state governments. Consensus on education was often tenuous and temporary, for every community had its factions, but without some agreement on purpose as well as practical matters like taxes and firewood, public schooling would have faltered.[2]

In the nineteenth century, American school board members constituted the largest body of public officials in the world. Elected trustees such as Darwin Atwater and the districts they supervised represented the standard form of face-to-face democracy in education. No other nation in the world has created such a decentralized system of public education, and no other nation has built such an inclusive and comprehensive system of public education. Local control and public support—the two characteristics are inextricably linked. Americans distrusted distant government and wanted governance of schools to be close to hand and transparent. Although there was plenty of conflict about schooling, people also believed in public education as a common good, a benefit which all could join in creating and in which all could share. Local citizens could vote for their representatives on the school board, participate in decisions, and deliberate about what was the best way to educate their children.[3]

Local control of public schools has appealed to citizens of many political persuasions, from the radical left to the radical right. A century ago Democrats and Populists were the people most loudly touting local self-rule. In recent years, local control, or "devolution," has become a mantra of Republicans in Congress and in state legislatures. Repeatedly, citizens have shown in votes and in opinion polls that they trust and respect local control and local districts far more than distant governments and distant schools. In 1992, 57 percent of Americans said that they wanted local school boards to have more control; only 26 percent wanted more federal control. They showed far less confidence in educational leadership by legislators in states and in Congress than in decision-making by local officials. The same was true during the nineteenth century, when citizens kept revising their state constitutions to prevent state officials from doing mischief. Not until after World War II has the federal government had any substantial impact on public schools through court decisions and legislation, and now it accounts for only about 7 percent of the funds spent on schooling (too much, say some conservatives in Congress).[4]

Despite the popularity of local control by elected trustees, elite policymakers in education have done their best to restrict or eliminate lay self-rule. They wanted professionals to run things and called that "taking the schools out of politics." They tried, in civics classes, to take the politics out of students. During the Progressive era, perhaps not coincidentally, smaller and smaller percentages of citizens voted in major elections. During the first half of the twentieth century, the leadership cadre in public education was composed chiefly of city and state superintendents, foundation officials, leaders in university schools of education, and professional and business allies. They radically reduced lay governance in rural districts by consolidating school districts in the countryside and abolished local ward boards (school committees in urban wards) in the cities.

Their escape from local democracy was breathtaking. They consolidated about nine out of ten rural districts, thereby eliminating their elected trustees as well. In cities they mostly eliminated local ward boards, and between 1890 and 1920 the average number of central board members in large cities dropped from twenty-one to seven. They often equated lay control not with democracy but with patronage, corruption, and incompetence. More important, they created a "corporate model" of urban school systems that fundamentally altered the ideology and practice of representative democracy in education. They thought of schools as quasi-businesses best run by experts. What was the point of lay participation in educational decision-making?[5]

The administrative progressives saw the first half of the twentieth century as a golden age of the professional leader and the corporate school, when school trustees and superintendents worked in tandem to run the schools and modernize education according to a professional template. From the middle 1950s onward, however, the prestige and power of local school boards eroded rapidly. The corporate model of governance in which experts were supposed to run things was ill suited to a new day when excluded groups demanded political participation and social justice. Some urban activists wanted to substitute community school boards for the central school boards, regarding the latter as unresponsive and part of the problem rather than the solution. The people elected to represent their communities in education—local school boards—faced an intense drumbeat of criticism all across the political spectrum. This is the way David Martin, editor of *The American School Board Journal,* summarized the accusations against school trustees in recent decades:

You aren't in the forefront of education innovation.

You spend too much time on trivia.

The public supports the idea of local control but doesn't really understand it.

Not enough of the right people serve on school boards.

School boards should be eliminated.[6]

Critics have periodically concluded—usually in times of social stress—that elected school boards and local districts were so ineffective and obsolete that they should be abolished. The educator Charles Judd, of the University of Chicago, argued in the 1930s for the abolition of local school boards, claiming that local control of schools by elected school trustees was an inefficient anachronism. Instead, he said, superintendents should run the schools, unencumbered by school boards that meddled with matters—such as the curriculum—that were best left to experts. Another critic concerned about professional autonomy, Myron Lieberman, wrote in 1960 that local control of schools was the main source of "the dull parochialism and attenuated totalitarianism" of American schooling. In 1956, amidst the Cold War, Admiral Hyman Rickover argued that the nation could never compete educationally with the Soviets if "the control and financing of schools is in the hands of thousands of local school boards." In 1991, the conservative critic Chester E. Finn declared school boards and their districts to be dinosaurs. They no longer raised the bulk of the school funds, lagged behind in reforms, were irrelevant to national or state standards, and hobbled school-site reform. People with different agendas, then, found local districts and school boards an apt target.[7]

Federal activists have not seen much point in school districts, either. The architects of Great Society programs regarded local school board members mostly as obstacles to reform, not as partners in liberal educational improvement. No members of local school boards were invited to the White House for the signing of the Elementary and Secondary Education Act (ESEA). Instead, the honored guests were the teachers' unions, foundation officials, and scholars associated with new federal curriculums in science and mathematics. In congressional hearings on helping poor children through ESEA, Senator Robert Kennedy asked, "Would you not agree . . . that one of the really great problems we have . . . is the school boards in some of these states?" Some New Frontiersmen dismissed local district leaders as stand-patters on racial segregation and insensitive to the needs of the poor. They were clearly out of the loop of federal policy formation, though they had to carry out federal mandates. School district trustees became, in Jacqueline Danzberger's phrase, "forgotten players on the education team."[8]

In their local districts, superintendents and school trustees saw local control constricted by powerful new forces. Militant teacher unions won collective bargaining. Federal and state laws freely legislated new mandates while often failing to fund them. Litigants took school boards to court on issues ranging from racial segregation to policies on student discipline. State legislatures mandated curricular changes, new tests, and higher standards for teachers. States threatened to take over districts in debt or in academic trouble because students continued to flunk tests. City school districts seemed unmanageably large and contentious, surely not the apolitical corporations their designers intended or the grass-roots democracy favored by Thomas Jefferson and advocates of local control.[9]

In recent years, when reformers have discussed national standards, state frameworks, and school site management, they typically have ignored local districts and their school boards. With some important exceptions, policy analysts in recent years have generally focused attention on every level of governance *but* local districts.[10]

Why is it that most citizens have trusted local control and local schools but cosmopolitan policy analysts and reformers have generally weakened, ignored, or disparaged local control, the traditional form of representative democracy in public education? What new forms of control and new conceptions of democracy did policy elites wish to substitute for the traditional elected local school boards? Clues to these puzzles lie buried in the complex history of

the transformation of the theory and practice of democratic control
of public schools.

Local Control of Public Schools in the Nineteenth Century

Districts like the one in Mantua Village, with its one-room school,
had a long political lineage and were entrenched in American society. Thomas Jefferson and starchy New Englanders might have
agreed on little else, but on the virtues of the town meeting form
of democracy they had a meeting of minds. Jefferson tried to persuade his fellow Virginians to divide up the state's counties into
wards (or groupings of about a hundred families) that would function like Yankee town meetings. Each ward would have its own
school and elected official to look after its welfare. Jefferson believed that such face-to-face small political units were seedbeds of
citizenship, small civil societies where adults as well as children
could learn how to exercise their republican duties and preserve
their rights and liberties. "The elementary republics of the wards,
the county republics, the State republics and the Republic of the
Union would form a gradation of authorities," he declared. John
Dewey shared Jefferson's belief that self-rule, the key to democracy, grew best in small, cooperative communities. Such educative
and transparent self-government was "the heart of [Jefferson's] philosophy of politics," wrote Dewey, and akin to Dewey's concept of
democratic practice.[11]

Jefferson never managed to persuade Virginians to create these
ward schools, but local control, carried by migrants from the Northeast, took root rapidly in the new states carved out of the public
domain in what is now the Midwest. Today an airplane passenger
flying over the prairie states can see the townships laid out by congressional ordinances in the 1780s but governed by locally elected

officials. The one-room school district persisted; as late as 1918 there still were over ninety thousand one-teacher schools in the Midwest, and in the nation as a whole almost half of schoolchildren attended such schools. In school district meetings, the historian Wayne E. Fuller observes, "both native and foreign-born Americans learned to participate in making decisions and took their first lessons in politics. Sides were taken and debated; arguments were won and lost. Elections, often hotly contested, removed some from office and elevated others to places of responsibility on the school board." Through such practices, "the mechanisms of democracy became almost second nature to them."[12]

One reason Americans chose *locally controlled* public schools is simply that the population was very scattered and rural. Other nations, however, have produced *centrally controlled* rural schools. The choice depended on their political cultures. In the United States, a powerful incentive for local control was the deep American distrust of distant governments, whether that of King George III or the federal government in Washington. In the nineteenth century citizens also tended to regard state governments as distant and prone to mischief. When they wrote and rewrote their state constitutions, Americans did their best, over and over again, to limit the powers of state governments. Some constitutions permitted the legislature to convene only every other year, for only a short time, and only to decide a limited set of issues. A delegate to the California constitutional convention in 1879 proposed—presumably tongue in cheek—that it be a felony to call for a session of the legislature. Phobias about nefarious doings in federal or state capitols are hardly new.[13]

One way to counter this distrust of distant governments was to elect local school trustees to run local districts. Then communities could retain collective decisions about schooling—who would teach, how much schools would cost, and what kind of instruction to offer. If district voters disagreed with school trustees, they could elect others. Citizens came to think it was their right to settle questions locally since they paid most of the bills and knew local circumstances. In the mountain town of Marble, Colorado, the local newspaper complained in 1916 about "the law which permits county commissioners to override the taxpayers of a school district and thwart their desires . . . It is a fine commentary on law when the taxpayers of a school district vote unanimously to tax themselves a certain amount in order to have superior educational advantages, and then three commissioners, sitting in solemn session over across a range of mountains, arbitrarily nullify the action without even so much as saying by your leave."[14]

But there was a puzzle about this American system: Even though the control of public schools was highly decentralized, the schools themselves looked surprisingly alike in message and form. A strong common ideology, more than state regulation, produced this Victorian-era standardization. In Europe, wrote a Swedish observer in 1853, ministers of education gave their fiats in "Egyptian darkness," but in the United States local schools depended on "the power of persuasion and on the activity of the people itself, when it shall have been raised to consciousness." This "consciousness" in education took the form of a pervasive common school ideology that taught that all citizens should receive sound moral and civic training. Public schools were to be responsive not only to parents but to the entire community. The education of all was a common good, and shaping and supporting this common good was a duty of all conscientious citizens. Common culture, more than common state command, helps explain the similarities between public schools across the nation.[15]

The term school *trustee* is revealing. Victorian orators argued that these elected representatives held in trust not only the education of

all the children of their community but also the future of the whole
society. School trustees, said Horace Mann, were responsible for
the duties "of improving the young, of advancing the welfare of the
state and of the race." Mann argued that school committeemen
should be aristocrats of character, exemplars of the values they
sought to inculcate in the children. They "are more worthy than
any other class of men, to be considered as the pilots, who are di-
recting the course of the bark that contains all the precious interests
of mankind, and steering it either for its rescue or its ruin." Mann
wanted more state regulation of schools, but he recognized that
even in the urban commonwealth of Massachusetts local control
was a firmly established tradition.[16]

In the middle of the nineteenth century, in cities as well as in the
countryside, school board members were expected to be, in Horace Mann's words, "the administrators of the system; and in proportion to the fidelity and intelligence exercised by them, the
system will flourish or decline." Even in cities that employed superintendents, conscientious school board members were expected to
attend to administration—selecting textbooks, approving the curriculum, contracting for schoolhouses and equipment, hiring teachers, mediating community conflicts over schooling—and they created
enough subcommittees to accomplish the work. One reason most
urban school boards were large was that trustees thought it took
many people to supervise the operation of large systems. Indeed,
when reformers in New York City proposed abolition of ward
boards and a reduction in the size of the central board, teachers
and community residents protested that so few trustees could not
possibly handle all the work or adequately represent all the ethnic
groups in the city. On cold days, asked one teacher, if there were
no ward trustees, who would check to see if there was enough coal
to keep the children warm?[17]

At first, patterns of governance of urban schools resembled those in the countryside and small towns. In Boston, for example, there were 190 committeemen who supervised that many small primary schools scattered across the city in the 1850s. As cities expanded, they added wards, each of which might have its own ward trustees to oversee the operation of local schools. Since ethnic groups clustered in different quarters of the city, often these elected ward school committees represented different immigrant groups. Central and ward school boards—and sometimes other agencies of government—fought over the perquisites and duties of office; the pattern of politics differed from city to city. In 1904 in Philadelphia there were 504 members of ward boards and 42 on the central board— a total of 546 trustees elected to represent the public interest and to oversee the administration of the schools.[18]

Elites considered such widespread participation by lay trustees not a virtue but a defect to be remedied. It led, they thought, to corruption and lay meddling in what should have been a professional domain. The machine politicians and the educators of immigrant stock had done enough damage. It was time to take the schools out of "politics" and turn them over to experts. Strategies for doing this varied between countryside and metropolis.[19]

The Consolidation of Rural School Districts

By the early twentieth century, professional leaders in education had come to agree that there were entirely too many school districts and too much grass-roots democracy. They had a name for the defect: "the rural school problem." Educational leaders of the first half of the twentieth century would have been astonished to find that school reformers today are turning to country schools as models of effective schooling. The administrative progressives re-

garded small rural districts as a problem-ridden sector of public education. Country schools were retrograde in large part because of
local control by laymen, "democracy gone to seed," said Ellwood P.
Cubberley. In the early days of the common school, he claimed,
the local district meetings might have "served as a forensic center
for the new democratic life of the time," but after the influx of immigrants unfamiliar with the republican way of thinking, those
meetings degenerated into petty politics.[20]

One answer to the "rural school problem" was to eliminate small
districts through consolidation, a strategy to restrict local control
and enhance professional autonomy. The consolidation of tiny
school districts radically reduced the number of rural school districts and put school boards at a greater distance from local neighborhoods. While the total population mushroomed from 1930 to
1991, the number of districts dropped from about 130,000 to
15,378. In 1930 there were about 150,000 one-teacher schools; in
1950, 60,000; and today, less than 1,000. Few reforms have ever
been so fully implemented. Michael Kirst estimates that in the
1930s "a typical school board member represented approximately
200 people; by 1970 . . . 3,000 constituents."[21]

The activists who sought to consolidate and standardize rural education found many faults in tiny districts and one-room schools.
Rural teachers tended to be young, poorly trained, and grossly un-
derpaid (the most capable instructors often migrated to large districts). Many schoolhouses were dilapidated, cold in winter and hot
in summer, and possessed only the most rudimentary teaching aids
(some even lacked textbooks). The curriculum was formal and narrow, said advocates of consolidation, and teaching by rote was
common. The local school board trustees, they thought, were apt
to be provincial if not ignorant, parsimonious if not outright stingy,
and incompetent in professional matters. Unfortunately, they gave

local patrons what they wanted: thin, cheap, and parochial gruel. Schooling prepared students neither to prosper as farmers nor to adapt to jobs in cities. Country schools should, but didn't, liberate children from the provincialism of their parents.[22]

People in rural communities dissented from such an indictment and fought consolidation in pitched battles from Maine to Oregon. The critics often took the worst schools as the average. In much of the United States, particularly the rural schools of the Midwest and West, one-teacher schools were reasonably well supported and effective, frequently graduating young people who were more literate than graduates of urban systems. As Wayne Fuller shows, such school districts often gave citizens skills and practice in face-to-face democratic decision-making in settings in which children could observe and learn political behavior from adults in the community. The young could also profit from the economic skills and social capital embedded in village life.[23]

Critics of rural education were often condescending and arrogant, but they did underscore and seek to remedy some deep inequalities in rural education. The biggest dividing line of educational resources was between schools in cities and those in the countryside. In impoverished regions—much of the deep South, Appalachia, and the Dust Bowl states, for example—families had to struggle hard to provide even a meager dose of schooling for their children. They could not pay for trained teachers or in many cases afford even desks and books. The gross underfunding of rural schools in such poor communities was the result of an impoverished tax base more than the product of stingy patrons. In the 1930s, farmers raised 31 percent of the country's children but received only 9 percent of the national income. Indigent rural families tended to have the most children. The poorest young people, who needed formal education the most, generally received the least. They were sometimes unable to meet even modest standards of literacy; many rural southerners, for example, failed mental tests in the draft for World War II.[24]

Not all rural families enjoyed an advantage cherished by most small school districts, self-rule. Blacks, Indians, and Mexicans generally did not exercise the sort of local control of public schools that was customary for rural white Americans. Black schools in the South were subject to white county boards and superintendents. Their students got a separate and grossly unequal education. The Bureau of Indian Affairs in faraway Washington, D.C., generally set the curriculum and managed the budgets of rural schools for Indians. Itinerant Mexican field workers' children attended rural schools only sporadically. Local white farmers ran the schools and often regarded the education of the field workers not as an entitlement but as a sometime charity. The Mexicans who did enter the classroom were apt to find that Anglo teachers and children stereotyped them and denigrated their culture. In the era of World War I even rural whites often faced draconian state-decreed methods of assimilation to "American" ways if they were immigrants. A Norwegian boy felt like an outsider in his one-room school: "Directly in front of him hung the blackboard; at the top of it was written in a beautiful hand, 'This is an American school; in work and play alike we speak English only.' He read the commandment twice; a feeling of shame came over him and he slunk even lower in his seat."[25]

At their best, however, and perhaps even at their average, rural schools were not quite the "problem" that the reformers complained about. Many themes of present-day reform are foreshadowed in country school districts: the virtues of smallness, a view of the school as a community and the community as a school, the responsiveness of schooling to the values and commitments of local citizens, and a lack of bureaucratic buffers between parents and teachers. All of these qualities lend meaning to "local control," a concept that has resonance for both conservatives and liberals today. Most important, perhaps, though largely unselfconscious, were the lessons taught about democracy. Today, some activists in cities and suburbs try to reproduce a kind of citizen participation that occurred spontaneously in rural communities when direct democracy and local control seemed synonymous terms.

And inside the classroom, many notions that seem new and progressive today were standard practice in America's country schools in the past: older children teaching younger ones, nongraded classrooms, flexible scheduling, and instruction that was personalized because the teacher knew the pupils as individuals. Obviously, not all one-teacher small schools had these virtues, but country schools had a potential that their critics ignored and a social vitality that continues to attract those who favor small schools and decentralization today.[26]

But the winners in the contest over consolidation of rural schools were the educators who lobbied for state laws to combine country schools and eliminate districts. Consolidation of rural districts was their crowning achievement. They worked to standardize curriculums on an urban model, to provide greater state financing, and to upgrade and supervise rural teachers. The reformers believed they were professionalizing and improving an unequal and retarded sector of the educational system while giving farmers' children access to a more cosmopolitan world. Once they had repaired urban schools, they wanted to offer the same equality of education that was enjoyed by city children. As the American population became more urban, so did the character of education, even in the hinterland.

Democracy without Politics

The administrative reformers of the twentieth century believed they knew what was wrong with urban education: The older concepts and forms of democracy had failed. Too many of the wrong people ran things—those immigrant politicians, for example, who wanted the schools to respect their cultures and hire their daughters as teachers. Lay school trustees tried to micro-manage the schools and to please their neighbors rather than to think of the city as a whole. Politics lurked around every corner and produced graft, favoritism, and inefficiency. Administration of schools should be done by professionals, but nobody would ever know that by observing the way schools were actually run.[27]

So first the administrative reformers and their allies wanted to "take the schools out of politics" by clearing away the political underbrush of patronage, abolishing ward committees, slicing the size of the large central boards, electing trustees at large rather than by district, and finding a way to attract "the better citizens" to the board. The result, they thought, would be democracy as it should be.[28]

The administrative reformers wanted to reduce the number of trustees and to elect men who were professional and business leaders in their communities. Reformers did not abandon the moral and personal qualities Horace Mann prescribed for the ideal school trustee, but they did add further prescriptions. They wanted board members to be "successful" men (not women), preferably business and professional leaders, well educated, and prosperous. Such trustees, said the U.S. Commissioner of Education, "have no personal ends to serve and no special cause to plead." They would control schooling not directly—that would be meddling—but indirectly, by selecting superintendents trained in "scientific management." They would know how to delegate the management of schooling to experts, who would be best qualified to understand and "really represent the interests of the children." Here was a shift in the concept of democratic governance of schools—not officials elected to represent constituents, or direct participation of citizens, or deliberative democracy, but decision-making by experts, a professional elite who knew what was in the best interests of the students.[29]

No amount of wishful thinking could have transformed the politics of education into neutral administration, for schooling is and has always been intrinsically political. The question is not whether politics but whose politics. As school board members came to be drawn more and more from the upper strata of their communities and as they turned over more decision-making to experts, the "reforms" restricted the kinds of choices citizens had exercised under an older, more localized, partisan, and pluralistic system of political control of city schools.

Even among superintendents, the group that presumably stood to gain most from the new system of district governance, a few had their doubts about the new elitism. The school chief of Omaha, Nebraska, argued that "we must remember that this is a representative government—a government by all the people, not by those we think are the best people; and we cannot always have members all of a kind who move in the highest circles of society . . . I am not sure but that the residents of 'Hell's Half Acre' are sometimes entitled to representation." He argued that "all citizens should be directly interested in the schools, and one of the best ways to have them interested is for them to have some voice in the selection of the men who manage the schools. The educative influence in the community of a general election of school-board members, in which general school policies are discussed, is good."[30]

The new corporate ideal of educational governance advertised itself as apolitical. The board of education operated in theory like the trustees of a bank, and the superintendent had the authority of a business CEO. The whole notion of representative lay democracy was wrong-headed in urban public education, thought Columbia president Nicholas Murray Butler. He told Chicago businessmen that he should "as soon think of the democratization of the treatment of appendicitis" as to speak of "the democratization of schools." "There is but one best way" of running schools, said a president of a school board, and this centralized and specialized system should be adopted everywhere. The public deserved to have its schools managed well—that was what the people should expect from democracy.[31]

The administrative reformers did not believe that they were abandoning democracy in public education. Quite the contrary, they thought that they were introducing a new and more efficient form of democracy suited to the new kinds of citizens filling the nation's cities. The corporate model of governance meant that school districts no longer needed to sway to and fro like tree branches in a windstorm. With the right people on school boards and professional experts determining what was in the best interests of the students, what room was left for politics?

As discussed in Chapter 4, the administrative progressives thought it a gross mistake to equate democratic instruction with exposing all students to the same curriculum. Considering the variety of students now attending city schools, Cubberley said, reformers should "give up the exceedingly democratic idea that all are equal, and that our society is devoid of classes." Instead, the new democratic education is differentiated enough to offer all students choices suited to their abilities and destinies. That was equality of opportunity. Differentiation designed by experts was the democratic way.[32]

If these reforms of urban public schools were designed to take the politics out of governance and the schools out of politics, that left a question: What to teach students about the political system? In the Progressive era state laws required more and more students to attend school and to take courses in civics or citizenship. But that was also a time of precipitous decline in the percentage of eligible citizens who voted in major elections. In her analysis of civics textbooks and curriculums of the time, the historian Julie Reuben discovered that lessons in citizenship stressed compliance with authorities, respect for expertise, and good behavior more than active participation in politics.[33]

Though it is hard to imagine today, when critics call large city systems ineffective, chaotic, and pathological, leaders at the turn of this century thought city school systems could lead the way for reform of the entire educational system. They planned and tested what today people call "systemic reform." Using "scientific" methods of curriculum-building, experts would determine what students should know and be able to do as adults, backward mapping from adult tasks and duties to the program of studies needed to prepare the young for "life." They believed that they had solved the problem of accountability by creating complex organizations in which responsibilities were clearly assigned to specialists. And finally, they developed complex systems of tests to appraise how well students had mastered the subjects they studied. Thus within city school systems they sought to align and institutionalize aims, standards, curricular frameworks, teacher education, and testing.[34]

The administrative reformers of the early twentieth century believed that if schools did a good job and tended to their public relations, citizens would be satisfied and would not politicize issues. The corporate model of governance proved to be so durable a feature of American urban school districts that political scientists of the 1950s sometimes referred to local school districts as "closed systems," mostly self-governing and highly stable in their routines. That was to change rapidly as social movements created by outsiders challenged this system in the name of political and cultural democracy.

The Old Order Changes

Although school politics seemed calm during the years from 1900 to 1950, leaders such as Thurgood Marshall were developing legal strategies to combat racial segregation. A number of social groups felt unheard and isolated on the periphery of school decision-making. They were typically treated as subjects, not citizens, of public education. In the last half-century the history of school governance is in large part the story of efforts to breach the buffers erected around schools and to make them responsive to new constituencies. Groups that felt excluded or unfairly treated—for example, African-Americans, Hispanics, the handicapped, women—organized in social movements and mobilized for political action. During the generation following the *Brown* school desegregation decision in 1954, many of these groups entered school politics at the grass-roots level, in state and national protest organizations and in the courts. In their campaigns for social justice in education they questioned democracy as rule by experts, sought to revive participatory democracy, and challenged and redefined issues of race, gender, and class. Besides employing traditional democratic beliefs and political strategies, they also expanded notions of democracy. They advocated, for example, cultural democracy, equal respect and equal rights for all groups.[35]

African-Americans organized the most powerful social protest movement yet to appear in educational history: the campaign for civil rights. Eloquent leaders such as Martin Luther King, Jr., at first mobilized black and white citizens by appealing to the common values of equality and social justice. In translating such an ideology into political demands black leaders tailored remedies for injustices to the particular circumstances they faced in different settings. They wanted more power over their lives and better education for their children. In the South, racial segregation of pupils, like disenfranchisement of their parents, was a target of protest because it denied the meaning of democratic citizenship. So black leaders confronted segregation head on in local communities and used the federal courts to overthrow the racial caste system. In northern ghettoes, by contrast, when school boards dragged their feet on desegregation, black activists often pressed instead for radical decentralization and community control.[36]

Other groups that had little voice under the old order—Hispanics, native Americans, women, parents of children with special needs—often used strategies similar to those of black leaders. On one point most activists in social movements agreed: Local school boards and bureaucracies were often unresponsive. Under the corporate model that allegedly took schools out of politics, administrators were praised for *not* being too responsive to "pressure groups" that wanted them to engage in "social engineering," although social engineering by educational experts was another matter.[37]

When local officials ignored their demands, activists pursued a variety of tactics. They took to the streets to protest, sought media coverage, lobbied the Congress and state legislatures for new laws, and litigated in federal and state courts. They found allies in the administrations of Presidents Kennedy and Johnson and in some state capitols. Through judges' decrees, legislation, and administrative regulations, they sought to secure rights and win entitlements long denied at the local level.[38]

Law offered a centralized lever to bring about change at the district level, profoundly altering the old balance of power when most decision-making rested with elected local officials. Federal courts in both the South and the North required laggard districts to desegregate the schools by race. Feminists used Title IX, passed by Congress in 1972, to desegregate schools by sex and to eliminate institutional sexism. Public Law 94–142 (1975) mandated services and classroom practices for the handicapped. In the *Lau* (1974) decision the Supreme Court required educators to provide services for non–English-speaking students, and through legislation and regulations the federal government and many states translated that mandate into programs of bilingual education. Activists in the War on Poverty targeted funds to students from low-income families and devised regulations to make sure that they reached poor children.[39]

These programs and others enlarged and complicated the role of the federal government and the states in the governance of education. Most reform strategies promoted centralization. At the same time, some protest groups wanted radical decentralization. Responding to demands for local participation in school decision-making, federal and state lawmakers sometimes mandated school-community councils to oversee new educational programs or decide school policies. Such school-based agencies strengthened the influence and participation of parents in individual schools but rarely altered the overall distribution of power. Not until the Chicago Public Schools implemented a plan to give substantial power to local boards in each Chicago school did any major district attempt to install a thorough form of "democratic localism."[40]

With the exception of the radical experiment in decentralization in Chicago, the educational establishment generally responded to the demand for community control by adding new layers of decentralized governance or new forms of "community participation" that were apt to be more symbolic than real. The result of all of this, more often than not, was a more elaborate and less coordinated bureaucracy—more the appearance than the reality of decentralized democracy. When New York decided to create thirty-two districts for its student population of over one million, its individual districts were typically the size of a medium-sized city.[41]

The intense social movements of the 1960s and early 1970s shook the old order of school governance, but the response of the establishment to their demands often did not produce a coherent new order. One way in which school districts and state and federal agencies responded to dissent was to bureaucratize it, to name the problem and to appoint a new administrator to take care of it. As John Meyer has noted, the bureaucratization of dissent and reform produced a fragmented form of centralization.[42]

"Accountability" became a cloak of many colors. Sometimes accountability just meant keeping track of federal and state aid. Another concept of accountability was responsiveness to the many protest groups that demanded attention to their agendas. Such responsiveness might take the form of introducing black history into the curriculum or appointing a Title IX coordinator to correct gender injustices. Accountability also became compliance with the legal mandates that resulted from new litigation in education, for districts had to respond to court-ordered racial desegregation, elimination of sex discrimination, and protection of procedural rights for students and teachers. Still another kind of accountability consisted of offering students more choices, as in elective courses or alternative schools, discussed in Chapter 6.

In the 1980s and 1990s the pendulum of policy swung to state-level centralization and accountability by test scores. States passed legislation to make students work harder by prescribing tougher courses, requiring children to go to school for longer periods of time, and seeking to ratchet up the system to "world-class standards" by imposing more and more tests.[43]

Success came to mean doing well on standardized exams. The

center of balance in public policy on schooling became economic success, individual and national. The economic rationale and the stress on the academic basics gave a degree of coherence of purpose after a half-century of turmoil and tensions. But what had happened to democracy in education—who needed it? After a century of weakening of local control, what work was left for elected local school boards to do?[44]

Recent Decades

The politics of education in the United States has never been more fluid and complicated than in recent decades. To illustrate, imagine that some shapers of educational policy in the past were to wake up in the millennial year 2001 as modern-day Rip Van Winkles, unaware of what has been happening in the meantime but remembering the triumphal reforms of their own lifetimes. They raise different questions about the present moment in reform of educational governance.

Horace Mann discovers that many key policymakers, including Presidents of the United States, think that schooling should be part of an open market in which parents choose, as consumers, where to send their children. What happened, asks the evangelist for the common school ideal, to the notion that public education is a common good? Do not all citizens have a stake in the civic and moral instruction of the next generation? And why, after many decades of toil to create schools for all children, do so many parents want to educate their children at home?

A board member of a one-room school of the 1890s—one of almost half a million elected lay trustees of American schools—awakens to find that there are fewer than a thousand one-room schools and that districts have been consolidated until there are fewer than sixteen thousand. School trustees don't seem to matter much any more. When people talk about improving schools, they discuss what the federal government and states should do but seem to forget about school district trustees. What's happened to local control?

Ellwood P. Cubberley wakes up to find that the Chicago of 2000 has outdone the Philadelphia of 1904 in participatory democracy, having 11 school board members for each of 542 schools. This rebirth of ward school committees is bad enough, he might exclaim, but even worse is the trend in big cities in the 1990s to turn control of schools over to mayors. Good grief, he might ask, haven't citizens learned from the past that those are paths to chaos and corruption?[45]

Pierre S. Du Pont, reorganizer of education in Delaware (as well as designer of General Motors and the Dupont Corporation), awakens to discover that business elites denounce centralization and bureaucracy as red tape and gridlock and call for "restructuring" in education as in business—by which they usually mean decentralization of decision-making to the school site. Do they know nothing about the value of scientific management, economies of scale, consolidation, and coordination from the top down?[46]

Over the years, school reformers have seesawed back and forth on issues of centralization and decentralization, but by and large the changes in school governance have narrowed the discretion and confined the powers of local school districts. The recent No Child Left Behind Act, discussed in Chapter 4, is a case in point. The federal government requires states to use a test-based accountability system to measure how school districts, individual schools, and children are performing academically. If students attend schools that fail to meet the test goal for two years, they are to be given the chance to attend better schools. This approach, of course, focuses educators' attention on test results as the prime measure of education and assumes that there are enough seats in good schools to meet the need. That is hardly the case in most urban districts. Los Angeles lacks 200,000 seats for the students who should be attending full time. "You just can't write a rule in Washington for this particular circumstance," says Los Angeles Superintendent Roy Romer. The No Child Left Behind Act, writes Richard F. Elmore, is "the single largest—and the single most damaging—expansion of federal power over the nation's education system."[47]

Until the middle decades of the twentieth century, public schools were mostly controlled locally, especially in rural and small town communities, where over half the students lived as late as 1920. As in Darwin Atwater's town, neighbors elected each other to do the work of school trustees. Rural and small town school systems were not just places for children to learn the Three Rs. They also were public spaces where citizens of all ages learned and practiced democracy in a familiar community setting. Education in self-rule took place in the public life that swirled about the common school and that taught how democracy worked (or did not). In school districts citizens elected trustees to *represent* them, had ample opportunity to *participate* in the life of the school, and could practice *deliberative* democracy by debating school policies.[48]

The local school district is still a basic building block of democratic school governance. Commitment to self-rule has been a key article of faith in educational decision-making. Today people continue to trust local control of schools more than national or state governments. In policy talk about reforming public schools local school boards have often been neglected, but that is unwise since it is in local districts that policy meets practice in the most direct way. If elected local school boards disappeared, something like them would probably need to be reinvented.[49]

I don't mean to romanticize local control of schools. Local school districts are not—and should not be—free-standing and autonomous agencies. They are the creatures of the states and serve broad national purposes, now as in Mann's time. Many districts have had a sorry record in achieving racial and gender justice, in serving economic classes equitably, and in respecting religious freedom and cultural differences. Federal and state action has been necessary to guarantee civil rights and liberties in education. In addition, only federal and state governments can remedy "savage inequalities" in financial resources between districts and between states. Whether control should be centralized or localized depends on the issue at hand.[50]

No one program to revitalize local control could possibly fit all districts. Districts are often homogeneous in class and ethnoracial composition and lack the diversity many seek in a common school. Local leaders may be parochial and punish dissent. School districts vary enormously in size, in resources, in their levels of conflict or consensus, and in professional sophistication. After a century of attacks on local control and consolidation of rural schools, the remaining American school districts are hardly monolithic. Half of all districts have fewer than a thousand students, while the top 5 percent of urban districts enroll almost half the students in kindergarten through the twelfth grade. Some favored school districts have at least as much educational expertise as do most state departments of education, while others are so far behind the curve of innovation that they do not even realize that there is a curve.[51]

Right now many local school activists and professional educators are acutely aware of external regulations that constrain local reforms. Some of the most important tasks of governance and revitalization of schools can still be done best at the local level. Consider, for example, engaging parents and other citizens more in the work of the local schools. In dysfunctional schools parents and teachers sometimes do battle over the children. One issue that never seems to get settled—and that may lend itself to mediation at the district level—is how to stimulate lay participation in the schools without undermining the autonomy and disregarding the savvy of teachers and principals. Parents often pull back from participation not because they lack interest but because they don't find anything important to do. When local citizens lose the sense that they can shape schools, its no wonder if they participate less in school affairs.

The answer to such problems is not, I think, more buffering of the school from critics and parents but creating forums for deliberating disputed issues. Often what originally sounds like single-issue politics of concern only to one interest group turns out to be an issue of broader concern. That discovery, in turn, can lead to ways in which professionals and volunteers can work together on school problems of mutual concern.[52]

Communication between local citizens and the professional educators of their school district may be especially helpful in launching and advancing educational reforms. If instructional reforms are to succeed in practice, local citizens and teachers need to understand and support the innovations. The public's notion of what constitutes a "real school" exerts a cultural brake on reforms that exceed the speed limit of pedagogical innovations. School districts should be open to new currents of educational thought and promising practices. They need to learn from expert outsiders. But districts, with their elected boards and professional staffs, also need to balance the cosmopolitan and the local, the traditional and the new, by relating educational programs to the goals and experience of local citizens.[53]

Trustees might conclude that the common sense of the community dictates doing "nothing innovative for a while," wrote a seasoned observer of local school democracy, "whatever the blandishments of reformers: After you go through a few cycles of tearing down walls for open classrooms and then putting them up again . . . or throwing out the old math for the new math and then pitching the new math for some version of the old math, you begin to recognize the virtues of being stodgy." This strategy may result in fewer reforms but a longer and happier life for those innovations that the community does decide it needs.[54]

And sometimes citizens and professionals together can preserve an endangered educational species—a lively arts program, for example—from a hasty relegation to the pedagogical wastebasket when fiscal retrenchment hits a school district. In educational deliberations we need conservationists as well as innovators.

As Darwin Atwater and many other trustees of common schools believed, a key job of leaders in education at the local level is to help communities achieve a sense of common ground in the education of children. All citizens, not just parents, have a stake in the civic education of the next generation. This principle, though deeply embedded in the history of democratic school governance, has often been neglected of late.[55]

CHAPTER SIX

Choices about Choice:
No Simple Solution

PARENTS and students thronged the auditorium of Martin Luther King, Jr., High School in the Upper West Side of Manhattan during the October High School Fair of the New York School Board. Recruiters from thirty-six high schools set up booths where they displayed their wares and dispensed calendars, cupcakes, and banners. People from specialized magnet schools advertised their programs. Families flocked around the booth of Stuyvesant High School at the center of the stage, learning about its admission test and its excellence in mathematics and science. Seward Park High School, one of the traditional neighborhood institutions required to admit everyone who came to the door, had its station at the end of the auditorium. Amid the competition for New York's students Seward Park had few obvious resources and faced disdain for its location on the Lower East Side. "Look at this," muttered a Seward Park English teacher, Jessica Siegel, when she looked about the hall, "Every kind of huckster thing." Here were the trappings of choice, observes Samuel G. Freedman, but underneath was "a system in which certain schools are engineered for success and others, like Seward Park, for failure."[1]

Not just at the High School Fair but also in national policy talk about education, *choice* has become a word to conjure with. It attracts presidents and governors of both political parties, business leaders and black activists, libertarians and conservatives, and educational progressives and traditionalists. But for every person who sees choice as the doorway to efficiency and equity, there are opponents who see it as a slippery slope for the public schools.[2]

Americans have always exercised some degree of choice of schools within the public educational system, but the present interest in choice is unprecedented. For over a century urban school districts have provided a marketplace of specialized vocational and academic high schools such as Stuyvesant. In the late 1960s and 1970s "alternative schools" flourished in public school systems, giving parents and students the opportunity to choose between different educational philosophies—"free schools," based on a libertarian pedagogy, were popular at that time, but they were later vastly outnumbered by private Christian day schools. School districts created magnet schools as a strategy for achieving racial desegregation. At the turn of the twenty-first century public charter schools attracted much attention. Self-governing and often providing a distinctive set of goals (or "charters"), they gain freedom from regulation by promising to improve instruction. These are only a sample of the forms of alternative education that have offered choices of schools within public education. The number of students in such schools, however, has constituted only a very small fraction of the total number of public school students. Today far more children are being schooled privately at home, for example, than are enrolled in public charter schools.[3]

Advocates of "schools of choice" within public education have argued that there is no one best type of school. They maintain that giving parents, teachers, and students a chance to create distinctive institutions produces greater parental commitment, more creative instruction by teachers, and more engagement of students with their studies. But although advocates of public school choice have sharply criticized mainstream public schools, they have rarely posed a radical challenge to the basic institution of public education.[4]

Some recent voucher advocates, by contrast, have mounted a basic critique of public education and called for a drastic remedy. "Government schools" have failed, they say, and the cure is to create an open marketplace in schooling by giving vouchers (scholarships) to all parents for their children's education in either private or public schools. These voucher advocates say that public education has become a "monopoly" that is wasteful, overregulated, unresponsive to captive clients, and shockingly inefficient. What is needed is competition between schools, both public and private, an open market in instruction in which parents can choose where to educate their children. If Americans shift from monolithic monopoly to a market economy in education, poor schools will wither from lack of patronage, and the number of effective schools will expand. As parents and students exercise choice, competition will winnow out the weak schools and reward the successful ones. As a result, test scores will rise and the United States will become more competitive economically.[5]

Choice, advocates of an open educational marketplace say, is as American as cherry/apple/blueberry pie (take your choice). Consumer sovereignty and the market have ruled in other domains. What is really surprising is not that citizens now want choice of schooling but that they have so long endured the public school monolith. Just patching a failed system will not do; a fundamental change in the funding and governance of schools is imperative. If parents could finance education with their children's' vouchers, or with tuition tax credits, the supply of fine schools would rapidly increase to meet the demand.

An educational marketplace would transform governance. If parents were able to choose schools, political problems would wither away. Instead of partisan squabbling and ever more bureaucratic regulation, a system of voucher-subsidized choice would empower families and cut red tape through radical deregulation. If people disagree, they do not need to accept unsatisfactory political compromises; they can select a school they admire and educators they agree with. The poor will benefit even more than the prosperous from such a system of choice, for they have lacked the political voice and the financial resources to take advantage of existing educational alternatives such as private schools or public education in affluent suburbs.[6]

Critics of the marketplace model of choice take issue with every point in these arguments, saying that it would undermine democracy in education and education in democracy.

For starters, calling public education a "monolithic monopoly" may be a good slogan, they say, but it is a murky conceptual guide for policy analysis. John F. Witte has documented the enormous variation between school districts in size; in class, ethnic, and racial composition of student bodies; in organization by grades; in curriculum and pedagogy, including the uses of testing; and in wealth. He also shows that the actual pattern of governance is far from being "a relatively simple, monolithic bureaucracy that is hierarchical and centralized." He demonstrates that the actual "control and influence systems"—composed of federal, state and local authorities, unions, organized interest groups, private vendors, professional officials and organizations, teachers, parents, students, and citizens—result in complex methods of decision-making that produce much variety in purpose and practice in public schools.[7]

How, ask voucher critics, could such a system be considered a monolith? Not only are public schools diverse in governance and funding but they offer an astonishing variety of choices of curriculum to individual students and their families. Over time, public schools have adapted in countless ways to the demands of their clients. If one compares the structure of centralized European educational systems and decentralized American schools, it becomes apparent that individuals have far more choices in the United States, where there are many points of entry and reentry and opportunities to shift between courses of study. American schools have added hundreds of new subjects to meet public demands. Choice, however, is hardly an uncomplicated good. Few people believe that all choices should be unconstrained.[8]

Some critics of vouchers argue against the marketplace model on grounds of democratic political philosophy. To construe education as a private consumer good bought in an educational marketplace impoverishes both education and democracy, they say. Publicly financed vouchers may give parents choices, but what about citizens who are not parents? What happens to collective decision-making and representative democracy in education? Education is not simply a consumer good but also a common good, like the air we breathe, because the way in which the next generation is educated affects the whole society. Political debate about education is not an annoying diversion from important matters; it has been a traditional arena for mediating differences and seeking common ground. If schools are judged solely on their success in attracting customers and producing good test scores, a catastrophic constriction of purposes could ensue. Treating schools simply as the product of marketplace forces subverts an essential democratic institution.[9]

The current debate about school choice engages the most fundamental questions about why we have schools, and how we can have good ones. But much of this controversy has been ahistorical, as if amnesia were a virtue (perhaps it is in polemics but not in policy). If one takes a long view of choice, the landscape changes. One needs to ask: Choice of *what* (of school, of courses, of elected representatives, of ethical climate?) Choice by *whom* (parents, students, teachers, voters)? Choice *for what purposes* (equity, liberty, efficiency, conscience, personal advantage, collective benefits)?

Choice in education, then, turns out to be a protean concept, changing over time and operating quite differently for different groups. I begin this inquiry into the history of educational choice by asking why nineteenth-century Americans, sluggish in providing most public services and highly suspicious of state government, mostly chose *public* and not private education for their children.

The next puzzle I examine is why about 10 percent of families chose to send their children to *nonpublic* schools? Were private school parents simply pursuing the best educational bargain in an open marketplace, treating education as if it were a consumer commodity? Or were private schools primarily organized around differences of conscience and culture, like most Christian day schools today? Indeed, is it even correct to say that most private school parents were exercising consumer choice, or is it more accurate to say that religious duty dictated the school their children attended?

Third, I explore how choice in education has sometimes not been a wise policy. Almost all observers of education agree that the public high school curriculum has given students broad choices, but they differ on whether that has improved education. I look at how the proliferation of elective courses has all too often trivialized and adulterated learning. If choice of courses has often led to low academic standards, and to inequities between social groups, why should choice of schools lead to high academic achievement and greater equity? What forms of choice—if any—would help the children left behind, the most underserved students today?

Finally, I reflect on how thinking of education as a consumer good might affect traditions of democracy in education and education in democracy.

Choosing the Common School

At the beginning of the nineteenth century Americans tended to regard schools and churches in the same light. Religion and education were both important, so it was proper to attend the church and school of your choice, and to pay for them yourself, if you could. There was a great variety of both schools and churches. The lines between "public" and "nonpublic" were not clearly drawn; hybrid institutions were common. Philanthropic organizations ran schools for the poor; elite schools catered to the prosperous; sectarian institutions abounded; girls from prosperous families learned feminine accomplishments in for-profit day schools; and so it went. Schooling at that time might be described as a miscellaneous marketplace for learning.[10]

In the first half of the nineteenth century it hardly seemed inevitable that public schools would trump private ones. A competitive entrepreneurial spirit among educators had created a healthy private education sector, and religious revivalism fueled the growth of sectarian schools of all types. As Michael Katz has shown, leaders experimented with a variety of ways to organize and control formal schooling, ranging from the "democratic localism" of the country district, to charity schools organized on a corporate plan, to incipient bureaucracy in city schools.[11]

By mid-century, however, more than half of children in school attended public schools and by 1890 about 90 percent of them did. Attempting to obtain more uniform and accurate statistics, the census in 1890 defined a public school as an institution "whose management was in the hands of public authorities, which was taught in a public school house by teachers selected by public officers and directly responsible to such officers." The common school became the school common to most American children. There was a shift from a general faith in education to a commitment to a particular kind of schooling, one that was publicly governed and financed. This ascendance of *public* schooling is puzzling, for Americans at that time tended to like markets and distrust governments.[12]

So, why did Americans choose *public* schools? As mentioned in Chapter 5, there were both practical and ideological reasons, and these often blended, as when voters demanded that school trustees be accountable to the citizens for public expenditures. The most common form of political control was democratic localism, the familiar theme of local control that has run through this book.

A single school for all children in the neighborhood made economic and social sense in the nineteenth century, when well over half of the population lived in rural areas (80 percent were nonurban in 1860, for example). Scattered one-room schools worked well when roads were poor and transportation rudimentary, when local citizens paid for schools mostly out of their own pockets, and when it would have been expensive, and sometimes impossible, to have separate schools for boys and girls, Baptists and Congregationalists, and the prosperous and the threadbare. In choosing to have a common school that would in theory teach a common denominator of all religions, Protestant Americans came close to disestablishing religion while establishing public education in its place.[13]

Pragmatic concerns go part way in explaining why nineteenth-century citizens chose public schools and elected their neighbors to run them. But the commitment to collective self-rule went beyond the lined ledgers in which school trustees kept their fiscal accounts. Democratic localism matched a widespread belief in democracy as representative government, preferably close to hand and transparent. When citizens made collective decisions in this way, they could show youth how collective choices worked (or did not) in a polity that prided itself on self-rule. In the nineteenth-century local majority rule decided many issues—say, about religious practices in the school or using a foreign language in instruction—that later would be adjudicated by the courts or set by state legislatures. There was little chance that state statutes would be enforced if local citizens disagreed.[14]

Conscience and Choice of School

While public education has predominated since the middle of the nineteenth century, about 10 percent of families have sent their children to private schools. Who were these citizens, and what did they want? Here, one might argue, is the place to investigate historically a question of interest today: How did the marketplace of choice in education actually work for the individual families who chose nonpublic schools? According to the model of choice now favored by many voucher advocates, parents might have been expected to shop around in the education market for the best academic product they could find at a price they could pay. No doubt, some parents did just that.

There is a problem with formulating the issue this way, however. As Thomas James observes, it is a mistake to construe "the world of private education as if it were only an amorphous market constituted by the free choice of individuals." Most parents who chose nonpublic education sought specific forms of religiously oriented schools. Such schools were typically the collective product of religious leaders and congregations who developed schools not to sell educational services to consumers but to teach religious doctrines and virtuous habits to their children.[15]

In 1890 about 8 percent of all students in elementary and secondary schools were enrolled in denominational or parochial schools, and about two thirds of those were in Catholic institutions.

In the twentieth century the percent of all students in nonpublic schools varied from about 8 to 14 percent, and eight or nine out of ten of them were in religious schools (most of these were Catholic).[16]

Most religious schools have been organized around differences of conscience and character. Indeed, if attendance was dictated by religious obligation, it may not be accurate to say that parents felt free to choose their children's schools. They felt it their duty to pass on to their children specific religious beliefs, which in some cases contradicted lessons taught in public schools.[17]

Some religious groups found it impossible to express their values as a religious and cultural minority within the public schools. Majoritarian choices about religious and moral education made by the trustees of the common schools effectively excluded them. Conscience and culture—a sense of obligation to preserve what one Catholic called "obedience for holy things"—were what parents in these groups cared about most. Trying to reconcile majority rule with minority rights of conscience has produced inevitable tensions in educational policy.[18]

The promoters of the common school clearly wanted to attract children from different walks of life and religious persuasions. Despite the sectarian and political conflicts that rent American society, they hoped to teach a noncontroversial but potent common denominator of civic and moral virtue. There was no more important educational goal than training upright citizens, and such moral instruction depended, they believed, on inculcating religious principles. "Education without religion," said an influential Protestant reformer, "is education without virtue."[19]

But was it possible to have a common religious basis for moral instruction when there were so many competing denominations? The answer was yes and no. Protestants generally said yes, because they could generally agree on the practice of reading the King

James Bible (regarded as Protestant) without sectarian commentary. Protestants often shared what Winthrop Hudson calls a "culture religion"; they identified the nation (or at least the Protestant
part of it) as literally God's country. Catholics generally said no; a
common faith was so watered down that it was no faith at all.[20]

Many Catholics considered the religious-moral teachings of the
common school an alien imposition. Their leaders held that reading
the King James Bible—even without comment—clearly violated
conscience and subverted priestly authority in interpreting the
Scriptures. As a religious minority, Catholics in Philadelphia pleaded
for constitutional protection in the midst of violent riots over the
Bible issue: "We are the minority; and for us, therefore, does the
Constitution exist. The majority need not its protection, for they
have the power to take care of their own interests . . . UNDER NO
CIRCUMSTANCES IS CONSCIENCE AT THE DISPOSAL OF A MAJORITY."[21]

Majorities in legislatures or on local school boards typically determined religious practices in the public schools, sometimes working out amicable compromises, as Benjamin Justice documents, but
sometimes triggering devilish combat. Courts generally deferred to
these elected officials when it came to questions of moral or religious instruction. In 1853, for example, the school board in Ells-
worth, Maine, ruled that all students must read from the King
James Bible or be expelled from school. The parish priest protested,
a group of children were expelled, and the priest opened a Catholic
school for them. A local mob then attacked the church and school
and tarred and feathered the priest.[22]

The father of a girl who had been expelled brought suit. The
Supreme Court of Maine dismissed the case, saying that a student
could not refuse to read "the Protestant version of the Bible" on
grounds of conscience or because the priest said that it was "a *sin*"
to read the book prescribed. "A law is not unconstitutional," de-

clared the Court, "because it may prohibit what one may *conscientiously* think right, or require what he may *conscientiously* think wrong. The State is governed by its own views of duty." So much for minority rights and the conscientious scruples of dissenting groups. There had to be an alternative to the common school. Many Catholic leaders insisted that it was the parochial school.[23]

American-born Protestant members of public school boards and Catholic leaders were often at loggerheads, unable to understand each other, much less to reconcile their differences, especially in cities. When Catholics tried to remove the King James Bible from the schools or to substitute the Catholic version, Protestants saw that as an attack on the moral foundations of the whole system. Members of the Know-Nothing Party organized politically to retain the Bible as a prime symbol of "Americanism." The pan-Protestantism of the common schools looked like a religious establishment to Catholics. Even when the offending Bibles, hymns, and prayers were removed, as they were in some places, the resulting secularized schools still did not satisfy Catholics, for ultimately they wanted a religiously based "true education," as opposed to "mere instruction."[24]

Catholic bishops and priests in the United States, many of them immigrants familiar with crusades against secularization and modernization in Europe, usually followed the lead of the Vatican in insisting that American Catholics must create their own schools as soon as they had the resources to do so. In the midst of virulent anti-Catholicism in 1852, the First Plenary Council of Baltimore *urged* local parishes to build schools, but the Third Council in 1884 *ordered* parishes to do so and held that parents had a religious duty to enroll their children. Despite some opposition from parents and priests, by the 1890s about 60 percent of parishes had fulfilled their religious duty to create a school, often at considerable financial sacrifice. Many Catholic immigrants—Germans, Poles, and

French Canadians, for example—used these schools to preserve not only their faith but also their languages and cultures.[25]

Duty compelled vast numbers of Catholics to abandon public schools and attend their own parochial schools, but that did not end ethnoreligious warfare. Indeed, in the 1870s regulating Catholic schools and giving state aid to parochial schools became explosive issues at the national, state, and local levels between Protestants and Catholics, Republicans and Democrats, and the native-born and the foreign-born. The issue of public aid to sectarian schools has periodically reemerged in heated debates, especially during the 1950s and in legal disputes today over vouchers used in parochial schools.[26]

Roman Catholics, of course, were not the only religious group to create a separate educational system as an alternative to the public school. Despite the general identification of Protestants with the common school, leaders and congregations in some Protestant denominations believed that they could preserve the distinctiveness of their faith and the cohesion of the faithful only by a "guarded," that is, separate, education. In justifying their own denominational schools they used the language of duty and collective action, not individual choice.[27]

Until recent decades, when evangelical Christian day schools expanded faster than any other segment of elementary education and became the largest body of Protestant schools, the largest numbers of Protestant schools were created by Lutherans and Seventh-Day Adventists. The conservative Missouri Synod of the Lutheran Church worked diligently to preserve doctrinal orthodoxy through its own schools. Lutheran schools, employing teachers who were "publicly and solemnly installed in the presence of their congregations," seemed to members "a self-evident and simple necessity." Orthodox Jews and black Muslims, as well, have created their own day

schools to provide a guarded education of their young and to ensure the religious and cultural survival of their groups amidst severe
discrimination.[28]

In the early twentieth century—as Catholics, Lutherans, and a
few other denominations continued to build their sectarian
schools—some Protestant fundamentalists became alarmed about
what they saw as growing secularism and liberalism in public
schools. No longer were they content to let local school boards rule
on religious issues such as Bible reading in the common schools—
that left too much to discretion. They wanted to legislate religious
practices and persuaded eleven states to *require* the reading of the
Bible in public schools. Political fundamentalism was linked to religious orthodoxy, for conservatives often mandated instruction in
patriotism as well as the biblical virtues. In the 1920s Oregon tested
how far the majority could invade minority rights of conscience
when it passed a referendum that would have forced all students
to attend public schools, thereby threatening the existence of all religious private schools (the U.S. Supreme Court overturned the
law).[29]

Two inescapable tensions in educational policy have been, and
are today, sharp policy disagreements about exactly what forms of
religious expression are permitted in the public schools and what
kind of assistance governments can give to sectarian schools. In the
1960s the Supreme Court banned prayer and ceremonial Bible
reading in public schools and debated what kind of public assistance could be given to religious schools. People generally agreed
that public education should promote morality and good citizenship, and accepted that this had some connection with religion, but
what connection? The Protestant flavor of the common school had
repelled many Catholics, and members of conservative Protestant
sects often regarded public school ethics as a marshmallow moral-

ity. The outlawing of the Bible and prayer encouraged many evangelical Protestants to band together to create Christian day schools because they feared that public schools would no longer welcome and buttress their religious values.[30]

Discussions of "choice" in education today often downplay the religious imperatives underlying the creation of most nonpublic schools. That is understandable because in many cities parents today, aided or not by vouchers, are selecting faith-based schools for their children independently of their own religious convictions. Black Protestants, for example, often send their children to urban Catholic parochial schools because they believe the education to be superior to that in urban public schools. But in the past most private schooling in America has originated not in a private search for the best academic value, but in collective moral actions of congregations and under the guidance of religious leaders. Such a collective vision of education is very different from a conception of schooling as a marketplace.

Choice in the High School Curriculum

The marketplace of education is sometimes compared with a shopping mall, with its multitude of "offerings" to choose from. But is the curriculum of endless choice a worthy model? One might think that advocates of school choice would applaud this marketplace within the school, but generally they do not.[31]

The influential education report of the Reagan administration, *A Nation at Risk,* declared in 1983 that the disarray—indeed, intellectual rout—in secondary education stemmed from "a cafeteria-style curriculum in which the appetizers and desserts can easily be mistaken for the main courses . . . this curricular smorgasbord, combined with extensive student choice, explains a great deal about where we find ourselves today." Individual choice of the many courses displayed in this cafeteria is bad policy, said the Reagan Commission.[32]

The proliferation of new subjects that became so suspect in the 1980s had begun as a reform in the early twentieth century, a time when high schools grew rapidly in size and complexity and student bodies grew more diverse. As discussed in Chapter 4, many groups outside the schools lobbied for additions to the curriculum: vocational and business tracks, "Americanization" classes, physical education—and so it went.

Even though much of the impetus for change came from outside the schools, educators were not simply passive brokers of outside interests. They had their own agendas even as they sought to accommodate what their constituents demanded. Some educators were eager to align the curriculum with the interests of potential dropouts. Some were advocates of the arts who wanted to develop students' creativity. Some specialized in vocational training and guidance. Although a few perceived that different curricular choices tended to segregate students by class, sex, race, and ethnicity, for the most part educators welcomed client choice of elective programs and courses as a convenient and ostensibly democratic way to respond to the great diversity of new students surging into the high schools.[33]

The range of curricular choices in high schools in recent decades is mind-boggling. In a survey in 1973, school principals listed over 2,100 different course titles, almost double those reported in 1961 and almost triple those of 1949. In 1961 there were 125 different course titles for mathematics alone. In the 1980s some large high schools offered more than 400 courses. As curricular labels proliferated, standardization of terminology declined; in 1973 only two course titles—English and first-year typing—were listed by 90 percent or more of high schools. In its statistical tables the federal government called secondary courses "offerings." The term is revealing, for over the past century high schools have increasingly become markets for merchandizing learning.[34]

In the 1960s the growth of electives in fields such as English and social studies eroded enrollments in courses that stressed a traditional canon. In 1961 84 percent of twelfth-graders took fourth-year English; in 1973 only 48 percent of them did, even though total enrollments in English, fed by electives, soared to 130 percent of the total number of students. The percentage of schools offering courses in sociology or social problems nearly doubled.[35]

By the late 1960s graduation requirements were modest to nearly nonexistent in many states, which allowed high school students considerable latitude to choose elective courses. In 1958 thirteen states had no required courses in English and nineteen had none in mathematics and science. In the late 1970s and increasingly in the 1980s, reformers at the national and state levels became alarmed about declines in test scores and called for a return to the "academic basics." One response was to impose stiffer graduation requirements, thereby regulating the academic marketplace of the high school. By the mid-1980s all but five states had imposed graduation requirements in English, mathematics, and science, and all but one state required courses in social studies; the average number of required years for each academic field increased steadily during the 1980s.[36]

Americans became disillusioned, then, with an increasingly unregulated and miscellaneous academic marketplace in secondary education. The first remedy for academic sloth was increased state regulation; then reformers called for national standards and possibly national testing. Had choice in an extensive elective system, after all, been a mistake? Was a consumer-oriented curriculum not a democratic way to deal with social diversity and with the multiple demands Americans placed on their high schools?

Choice of courses in the abstract was not necessarily good or bad. It depended in part on the quality of the courses—freedom to select junk-food courses was hardly admirable, but elective courses at their best gave teachers and students the opportunity to pursue challenging subjects in new ways. But high demand did not guarantee intellectual quality, since students often chose easy or faddish subjects rather than ambitious courses. In the early 1920s George Counts asked over eight hundred teachers what types of courses students elected; over half replied "the easier subjects." Under such a regime, David K. Cohen observes, "we can see that student choice within a curriculum that offered varying levels of difficulty would push out harder courses with easier ones."[37]

The new conventional wisdom about curriculum holds that governments—states and local school boards—should require students to take certain courses; this policy restricts their freedom in choosing courses. Advocates of a market system of schooling, by contrast, argue that choice of schools would lead to greater academic rigor and higher test scores. Is this incongruous? Recent research on high schools, Richard Elmore notes, shows that "student choice [of courses] functions to reinforce a mediocre, substandard level of academic content and performance, rather than raising that level." What assurances would there be, then, that students and their families would select rigorous *schools* if, when given the chance, they so often pick the less nutritious *courses* in the high school cafeteria?[38]

Another concern is this: Does a curricular marketplace result in subtle forms of unequal education, disguised because individuals are supposedly all free to "choose"? Theodore Sizer observes that "there is generosity in the expansive American high school, a place in which every interest and taste is respectfully accommodated and from which everyone (or almost everyone) graduates as virtual, symbolic equals." On the surface this is an admirable populism. But he points out that the high school's "riotous eclecticism—of standards as well as programs—has had and continues to have troubling consequences." Choice often turns out to be not a neutral device but a disguised social filter.[39]

Students' class background, gender, ethnicity, and race profoundly shaped their enrollment in elective courses and programs. Girls, for example, had far fewer choices than boys if they wanted vocational training, and whites had more options than blacks. The choice of curricular tracks of notably different quality—academic versus general, for example—has reflected the class backgrounds of students. And Cohen notes the irony that "the students who were supposed to have the greatest capacity for schoolwork were permitted the least freedom to choose, while those who were supposed to have the least academic capacity were permitted the most choices."[40]

The value of choice of high school courses has depended heavily on the quality of information available to students and families: Did teachers, parents, counselors, and fellow students give good advice? Misinformed choices made at one time have often limited later opportunities, as when students discovered too late that they had not taken the courses they needed to win admission to college or to prepare themselves for an occupation. Good information in selecting *schools* is even more important than choosing *courses* in a high school, yet as Elmore says, "high quality information about the content and performance of schools is difficult and costly to get; it must be collected with care, and it must be interpreted with detachment and skepticism after it is collected because it presents a limited picture of what schools are about." He points out that providers marketing their schools have "strong incentives . . . to promote their product, and to present superficial or inaccurate information on effectiveness."[41]

At the very time when some Americans find choice a magical motto when it means picking a school, others have come to question choice as it has actually operated. Why should one suppose that choice of schools in an academic marketplace would help those who need a solid education the most?[42]

Choice: A Protean Concept

There are many choices to be made about "choice," and there is no one correct answer for all circumstances.[43]

When voucher advocates today speak of school choice, they usually have in mind individual families choosing where to send their children to school. They envisage an education marketplace in which the consumer picks from an array of schooling options (and the public pays the bill). They seem to have little idea of what a radical break this would be not just with the American tradition of public schooling but with more than a century of private religious schooling as well.

Indeed, choice in American education has long meant something else—not parents making individual choices but communities making collective choices about schooling, by electing (choosing) school boards that set educational policy, and by voting school budgets and bonds up or down. Americans became convinced that the education of the community's children should be the concern of all citizens, not parents alone. And ever since, community by community, they have been making collective choices about how best to provide that education.

From early on, about 10 percent of parents have sent their children to private rather than public schools. Yet there, too, education has mostly reflected collective choices. About nine out of ten private school students attended denominational and parochial schools where the religious convictions and cultural values of the group were reinforced, not simply tolerated. They believed that they could preserve the distinctiveness of their faith and the cohesion of the faithful only by giving their children what the Lutherans called a "guarded education." The nature of these schools, and even the decision to attend one, had more to do with collective religious duty than individual consumer preference.

So where would one go to find an example of an academic marketplace full of consumer choices? What comes closest is the American public high school, where individual students have had a broad choice of course offerings. But ironically, this is a marketplace that advocates of school choice often dismiss as frivolous.

There are hundreds of thousands of children who attend dismal public (and yes, private) schools. In theory, providing vouchers to subsidize education might generate thousands of new and effective schools in impoverished communities, where they are most needed. But will there be enough good schools to escape to? It's no easy matter to create and preserve fine schools—that task takes time, energy, funding commitment, and professional savvy. Also, alternative schools, like small businesses, have had a high mortality rate. Even if vouchers and a new marketplace for schools could create many good new schools, would the most needy children end up in these good schools? Competition for a scarce resource—fine schools— between families that start out highly unequal in information, influence, and resources seems hardly likely to benefit the have-nots as much as the haves.[44]

But citizens need to start somewhere to ensure that the neediest children have decent schools. A jolt to the public school system—in the form of more parental choice of public schools—may help to bring about change. Advocates of charter schools, for instance, argue that more choice of schools could help loosen bureaucratic gridlock, encourage more democratic governance, develop more imaginative and compelling ways of honoring diverse values and cultures, and produce higher academic achievement.

There are promising examples of how parental choice and collective decision-making by parents, teachers, and administrators can improve the education of needy students. District 4 of New York City in Spanish Harlem, for example, was near the bottom of the city in academic performance in the early 1970s and ranked eighth in the number of welfare families among the twenty-sixth poorest districts of New York. Seymour Fliegel writes that the leaders of District 4 "chose to take risks and be innovative, in part because it had nowhere to go but up." Believing that good schools are organic, created from within by educators and parents with a distinct vision, reformers started building alternative schools one by one, beginning with a school for "acting out" students and one for study of the performing arts.[45]

Central Park East (CPE) attracted innovative teachers from the district and across the city under the leadership of Deborah W. Meier. As time passed, other teachers and principals designed alternative schools, many of them small and occupying only a part of a school building (CPE and Meier sought to distinguish between a "school" and a "building," thereby creating smaller communities of teachers and students). In a decade there were fifty-one schools in twenty buildings and all junior high schools became schools of choice. Parents were asked to choose three alternatives; 90 percent of them obtained one of their choices.[46]

The results of such reforms were impressive. District 4 climbed to the middle range of performance among the city's districts in mathematics and reading, and the number of junior high graduates admitted to selective high schools rose from ten to more than two hundred and fifty. Teachers, given much greater freedom, developed innovative academic programs. They stressed democratic forms of decision-making. "While public education may be useful as an industrial policy," said Meier, "it is *essential* to healthy public life in a democracy."[47]

District 4 offers one example of how greater choice for parents and more autonomy for teachers can reinvigorate inner-city schools academically and expand and deepen the meaning of democracy in education. If employed within the democratic structure and purposes of public education, choice can be one tool among many to expand opportunities for those, like the people of East Harlem, who have been denied a fair chance to learn. But choice is no panacea.[48]

At its best, public education has allowed citizens to make choices about schools that reflect what works not just for the individual but also for the community. Metaphors of the market should not obscure the full range of educational choices before citizens today.

Reflections

ALTHOUGH Adlai Stevenson believed that public education was "the most American thing about America," many people do not share that view today. Some citizens speak of "government schools" as if they were alien invaders of their communities instead of long-standing neighborhood institutions. At the turn of the twentieth-first century, people talk about the cash value of schooling or the latest innovation but rarely speak about the powerful ideas that link public schooling to our political past and future.

Daily, new get-smart-quick schemes to reform the schools pop up. Pupils should address teachers as "ma'am" and "sir." School-children should wear uniforms. School districts can raise money by giving Coca-Cola exclusive rights to tout and sell its sodas on campus. Students should fill in the proper bubbles on their standardized tests with no. 2 pencils, and if they don't, they should repeat the grade. Social promotion is out; nonsocial nonpromotion is in.

For more than a century public schools have been robust institutions, able to survive war, depressions, massive demographic changes, and even reformers. Amidst these trials, people retained a strong sense that education was part of the answer to problems, not the problem itself. But in recent decades, as schools have been drawn into the vortex of many social and political conflicts, and as an ideology of privatization has rapidly spread, doubts have arisen. Has public education failed the nation? Or, perhaps, has the nation failed education? The political and moral purposes that gave resonance to public education in earlier times have become muted, and constituencies that once supported common schools have become splintered and confused about where to invest their educational loyalties.

I am a partisan for the public schools—albeit a *critical* one, as this book indicates. I do not argue that public schools do a better—or worse—job than private schools in educating citizens (in any case we never have enough good schools, public or private, for the students who need them). But I believe that public schools represent a special kind of civic space that deserves to be supported by citizens whether they have children or not. The United States would be much impoverished if the public school system went to ruin. And one way to begin that impoverishment is to privatize the *purposes* of education.

The size and inclusiveness of public education is staggering. Almost anywhere a school-age child goes in the nation, she will find a public school she is entitled to attend. Almost one in four Americans work in schools either as students or staff. Schools are familiar to citizens as places to vote and to meet as well as places to educate children. Schools are more open to public participation in policymaking than are most other institutions, public or private. Once the most numerous public officials in the world—before consolidation of school districts—district trustees still represent the citizens who elected them to guide public education. When local citizens deliberate about the kind of education they want for their children, they are in effect debating the futures they want. Participation, representation, deliberation—these help to make schools places where adults can exercise their obligations as citizens.

In this book I have examined three issues in the creation of this civic space. The first is how leaders sought to educate republican citizens. The second is how they dealt with social diversity. And the third is ways of governing schools. A common theme runs through each of these topics: the search for common ground amid controversy and ethnoreligious diversity.

This history is in part a tale of persistent conflicts of values and policies. Whose values should be taught, whose history learned? Are pupils basically the same or different? To what degree should schooling be the same for all or differentiated? How should one diagnose and remedy academic failure? To what degree should school governance be centralized? Should experts or lay people govern the schools? Seen in the long view, such conflicts never seem truly settled, and for that reason I have called them unavoidable tensions. When you mix together common schools, a diverse society, and an open political system, you can expect disagreement and conflict. Occasionally, groups have engaged in winner-take-all policy combat, especially on heated issues such as Bible reading in the nineteenth century or racial desegregation in the 1960s.

But in the civic space occupied by public education, a political culture favoring accommodation and mediation has been common. For over a century, public schools have had a public mandate to teach children about civic and moral life. Horace Mann thought that school officials could avoid controversy in civic education by teaching only those civic and moral lessons on which everyone agreed—a common denominator. But often one person's unquestioned truth was another's sectarian myth or partisan story. Mann's

solution of noncontroversial virtue worked best in socially homogeneous communities where citizens agreed on most moral and
civic questions.

In socially diverse places the common ground in school policies
was often procedural, a willingness to follow democratic rules in
arriving at decisions. At its best, school governance was itself educational, as citizens debated with one another about how the community should educate the next generation.

Part of the deliberation, compromise, and reframing of issues
needed in educational policy requires balancing the claims of innovation and conservation, looking both forward and backward. It
is important to moderate the pendulum swings of fashion in policy
that decree that schools should be larger (or smaller), that more (or
fewer) courses should be elective, or that governance should be
more (or less) centralized. Another important—and often neglected—job in educational politics and policy is to conserve what
works in schools. There is no shortage of innovators with sure answers to educational problems. But when these reformers want to
transform educational practices, few ask what might be lost in the
process.

The word "conservationist" has an honorable ring when citizens
struggle to preserve unspoiled habitats or fine old buildings. When
real estate developers propose paving over wetlands, environmen-
tal activists are praised for stopping them. When people work to
conserve what is good in education, however, they are often dismissed as mossbacks or stand-patters. Government requires envi-
ronmental impact statements for construction projects—but not
student and teacher impact reports for educational reforms. Who
will defend endangered species of good schools, or good educational programs, from the relentless, if zig-zag, march of educational
progress?

It is easy to become so preoccupied with what is not working—the cacophony of bad schools—that one forgets what makes many schools sing. Good schools are hard to create and nurture, for they require healthy relationships of trust, challenge, and respect, qualities that take time to develop. These values become embedded in institutions as part of the common ground that unites the members of the schools. When teachers, students, parents, and administrators create such schools, it's important to preserve what makes them work, to sabotage ignorant efforts to fix what ain't broke, and to share knowledge about how to create more good schools.

Decisions about schooling are made in many places—in the White House and the courthouse, the Congress and the state legislature, the blue-ribbon committee of business leaders and the teachers' lounge. Jefferson argued that there was no better school of citizenship for both adults and the young than deliberating about common needs and values in a face-to-face community. His model of educational governance was a town meeting; people could learn democracy by practicing it. I think there is still a good case for vesting decisions about education, as much as possible, with the people who have to live directly with the results of those decisions, in local districts and even in individual schools.

Democracy is about making wise collective choices. Democracy in education and education in democracy are not quaint legacies from a distant and happier time. They have never been more essential to wise self-rule than they are today.

Notes

1. Schools for Citizens

1. Jefferson to William C. Jarvis, September 28, 1820, in Paul L. Ford, ed., *The Writings of Thomas Jefferson* (New York: G. P. Putnam Sons, 1899), vol. 10, p. 161; Charles Z. Lincoln, ed., *State of New York: Messages from the Governors . . . to and including the Year 1906* (Albany: J. B. Lyon Co., 1909), vol. 2, p. 1100; Horace Mann, *Twelfth Annual Report*, p. 78, as quoted in Lawrence A. Cremin, ed., *The Republic and the School: Horace Mann on the Education of Free Men* (New York: Teachers College Press, 1957), pp. 15, 14.
2. David Tyack, "Forming the National Character: Paradox in the Educational Thought of the Revolutionary Generation," *Harvard Educational Review* 36 (Winter 1966): 29–41.
3. Merle Curti, *The Social Ideas of American Educators* (New York: Charles Scribner's Sons, 1935); Larry Cuban and Dorothy Shipps, eds., *Reconstructing the Common Good in Education: Coping with Intractable American Dilemmas* (Stanford: Stanford University Press, 2000); Rush Welter, *Popular Education and Democratic Thought in America* (New York: Columbia University Press, 1962).
4. Jonathan Messerli, *Horace Mann: A Biography* (New York: Knopf, 1972); Mary Mann, *Life of Horace Mann* (Boston, 1865); Thomas James, "Rights of Conscience and State School Systems in Nineteenth Century America," in Paul Finkelman and Stephen E. Gottlieb, eds., *Toward a Usable Past: Liberty under State Constitutions* (Athens, Ga.: University of Georgia Press, 1991); Charles Leslie Glenn, Jr., *The Myth of the Common School* (Amherst, Mass.: University of Massachusetts Press, 1988).

5. Carl F. Kaestle, *Pillars of the Republic: Common Schools and American Society, 1780–1860* (New York: Hill and Wang, 1983), ch. 5; David Tyack and Elisabeth Hansot, *Managers of Virtue: Public School Leadership in America, 1820–1980* (New York: Basic Books, 1982), pt. 1.

6. Michael B. Katz, *The Irony of Early School Reform: Educational Innovation in Mid-Nineteenth Century Massachusetts* (Cambridge: Harvard University Press, 1968); James W. Fraser, *Between Church and State: Religion and Public Education in a Multicultural America* (New York: St. Martin's Press, 1999).

7. Tyack and Hansot, *Managers of Virtue*, pt. 1; Cuban and Shipps, eds., *Reconstructing the Common Good.*

8. Benjamin Justice, "Peaceable Adjustments: Religious Diversity and Local Control in New York State Public Schools, 1865–1900" (Ph.D. diss., Stanford University, 2002); Wallace D. Farnham, "The Weakened Spring of Government: A Study in Nineteenth Century American History," *American Historical Review* 68 (1963): 662–680.

9. Tyack, "Forming the National Character," pp. 29–41; portions of this chapter are adapted from that study; Frederick Rudolph, ed., *Essays on Education in the Early Republic* (Cambridge: Harvard University Press, 1965).

10. Andrew Lipscomb and Albert E. Berg, eds., *The Writings of Thomas Jefferson* (Washington, D.C.: Thomas Jefferson Memorial Association of the United States, 1903), vol. 10, p. 319; Jefferson on literacy quoted in Lorraine Smith Pangle and Thomas L. Pangle, *The Learning of Liberty: The Educational Ideas of the American Founders* (Lawrence: University Press of Kansas 1993), p. 115 (emphasis added); on ideological rather than ethnic criteria for identity, see Philip Gleason, "American Identity and Americanization," in Stephan Thernstrom, ed., *Harvard Enclycopedia of Ethnic Groups* (Cambridge: Harvard University Press, 1980), pp. 32–33, 31–58.

11. Lyman H. Butterfield, ed., *Letters of Benjamin Rush* (Princeton: Princeton University Press, 1951) vol. 1, p. 388; Harry R. Warfel, *Noah Webster: Schoolmaster to America* (New York: The Macmillan Co., 1936) p. 285; Allen O. Hansen, *Liberalism and American Education in the Eighteenth Century* (New York: The Macmillan Co., 1926).

12. "An Ordinance for Ascertaining the Mode of Disposing Lands in the Western Territory," May 20, 1785, *Journals of the American Congress, 1785* (Washington, D.C.: Way and Gideon, 1823), p. 520; Northwest Ordinance of 1787 quoted in Charles Kettleborough, ed., *Constitution Making in Indiana: A Sourcebook,* 3 vols. (Indianapolis: Indiana Historical Commission, 1916), vol. 1, pp. 31–32.

13. David Tyack, Thomas James, and Aaron Benavot, *Law and the Shaping of*

Public Education, 1785–1954 (Madison: University of Wisconsin Press, 1987), chs. 1–2.

14. Robert Wiebe, *The Opening of American Society: From the Adoption of the Constitution to the Eve of Disunion* (New York: Knopf, 1984), pp. 7–20; U.S. House of Representatives, Committee on Public Lands, "Report on Educational Land Policy," Feb. 24, 1826, as published in *Barnard's American Journal of Education* 28 (1878): 939, 942, 944; J. Ross Browne, *Report of the Debates in the Convention on the Formation of the State Constitution [in California] in September and October, 1848* (Washington, D.C.: J. T. Towers, 1850), pp. 18, 210; *Congressional Globe,* 40th Congress, 1st Session, March 16, 1867, pp. 166–167.

15. Elisabeth Hansot, "Civic Friendship: An Aristotelian Perspective," in Cuban and Shipps, eds., *Reconstructing the Common Good* pp. 173–185; Washington quoted in Edgar W. Knight, ed., *A Documentary History of Education in the South before 1860* (Chapel Hill: University of North Carolina Press, 1950), vol. 2, p. 4—also see pp. 17, 21–22; Julian P. Boyd, ed., *The Papers of Thomas Jefferson* (Princeton: Princeton University Press, 1950–) vol. 8, pp. 636–637.

16. Noah Webster, *The American Spelling Book* (Boston, 1798), pp. 154–155, 145–152; Ruth Miller Elson, *Guardians of Tradition: American Schoolbooks of the Nineteenth Century* (Lincoln: University of Nebraska Press, 1964).

17. Noah Webster, *A Collection of Essays and Fugitive Writings on Moral, Historical, Political, and Literary Subjects* (Boston, 1790), pp. 3, 17–21, 23, 25; Rush as quoted in Harry Good, *Benjamin Rush and His Services to American Education* (Berne, Ind.: Witness Press, 1918) p. 61 (emphasis added).

18. Gordon C. Lee, ed., *Crusade against Ignorance: Thomas Jefferson on Education* (New York: Teachers College Press, 1961), pp. 66, 97–100; for John Dewey's selections and commentaries on Jefferson, see Dewey, ed., *The Living Thoughts of Thomas Jefferson* (New York: Premier Books, 1957).

19. Lipscomb and Berg, *Jefferson,* vol. 12, p. 456; Leonard W. Levy, *Jefferson and Civil Liberties: The Darker Side* (Cambridge: Harvard University Press, 1963), p. 146; for a justification of Jefferson's attempted prescription of textbooks, see Arthur Bestor's argument in *Three Presidents and Their Books* (Urbana: University of Illiois Press, 1955), pp. 12–35, 39–44.

20. Jefferson to Governor John Tyler, May 26, 1810, quoted in Garrett Ward Sheldon, *The Political Philosophy of Thomas Jefferson* (Baltimore: The Johns Hopkins University Press, 1991), pp. 71, 60–82; James Bryant Conant, *Thomas Jefferson and the Development of American Public Education* (Berkeley: University of California Press, 1962).

21. Benjamin Rush, *A Plan for the Establishment of Public Schools and the Diffusion of Knowledge in Pennsylvania, to Which Are Added Thoughts upon the Mode of Education, Proper in a Republic* (Philadelphia: Thomas Dobson, 1786) pp. 14, 27, 20–22.

22. Horace Mann, *Life and Works of Horace Mann* (Boston: Lee and Shepard, 1865–1868), vol. 4, pp. 345, 354–356.

23. Calvin Stowe in *Transactions of the Fifth Annual Meeting of the Western Literary Institute and College of Professional Teachers* (Cincinnati: Executive Committee, 1836), pp. 75, 66–82.

24. John Higham, "Hanging Together: Divergent Unities in American History," *Journal of American History* 61 (1974): 13–14; Tyack and Hansot, *Managers,* pt. 1.

25. John Swett, *Methods of Teaching: A Hand-book of Principles, Directions, and Working Models for Common-school Teachers* (New York: American Book Co., 1885), p. 21, ch. 10; Steve Farkas and Jean Johnson, *Given the Circumstances: Teachers Talk about Public Education Today* (New York: Public Agenda, 1996).

26. Cremin, ed., *Republic and the School,* pp. 97, 94–97.

27. Bessie Pierce, *Public Opinion and the Teaching of History,* p. 29, chs. 1–2.

28. Stanley W. Lindberg, *The Annotated McGuffey: Selections from the McGuffey Eclectic Readers, 1836–1920* (New York: Van Nostrand Reinhold, 1976); David Tyack, ed., *Turning Points in American Educational History* (Waltham, Mass.: Blasdell Publishing Co., 1967), p. 178.

29. Wallace D. Farnham, "The Weakened Spring of Government: A Study in Nineteenth Century American History," *American Historical Review* 68 (1963): 662–680; the German immigrant Carl Schurz as quoted in George Fredrickson, *The Inner Civil War: Northern Intellectuals and the Civil War* (New York: Harper & Row, 1965), p. 8.

30. Justice, "Peaceable Adjustments"; James, "Rights of Conscience," pp. 117–147; the intense localism of American education is apparent in the census study by James H. Blodgett, *Report on Education in the United States at the Eleventh Census: 1890* (Washington, D.C.: Government Printing Office, 1893).

31. Robert Baird, *Religion in America* (New York: Harper and Brothers, 1844); Bessie Pierce, in *Civic Attitudes in American School Textbooks* (Chicago: University of Chicago Press, 1930), p. 85, gives an illuminating account of an anti-Catholic riot in a textbook read by parochial school students.

32. Kaestle, *Pillars,* ch. 7; Fraser, *Church and State.*

33. Thomas Nast, cartoon of "The American River Ganges," *Harper's Weekly,* April 1871; Robert D. Cross, "The Origins of the Catholic Parochial

Schools in America," *American Benedictine Review* 16 (1965): 194–209; Vincent Lannie, *Public Money and Parochial Education: Bishop Hughes, Governor Seward, and the New York School Controversy* (Cleveland: The Press of Case Western Reserve University, 1968); National Center for Educational Statistics, *120 Years of American Education: A Statistical Portrait* (Washington, D.C.: Government Printing Office, 1993).

34. Kansan quoted in James Carper, "A Common Faith for the Common School? Religion and Education in Kansas, 1861–1900," *Mid-America: An Historical Review* 60 (1978): 149–150.

35. Isaac Hecker, "Unification and Education," *The Catholic World* 13 (1871): 6, 1–14.

36. Robert Ulrich, "The Bennett Law of 1889: Education and Politics in Wisconsin" (Ph.D. diss., University of Wisconsin, 1965).

37. Joshua Fishman, *Language Loyalty in the United States* (The Hague: Mouton, 1966), pp. 234–236.

38. Harris quoted in *St. Louis School Report for 1875,* pp. 114–15, 11–13; Lloyd Jorgenson, *The Founding of Public Education in Wisconsin* (Madison: State Historical Society of Wisconsin, 1956), p. 145; Tyack, James, and Benavot, *Law,* pp. 170–171; Selwyn Troen, *The Public and the Schools: Shaping the St. Louis System, 1838–1920* (Columbia: University of Missouri Press, 1975).

39. National Education Association, *Addresses and Proceedings, 1891,* pp. 294–297; Tyack and Hansot, *Managers,* pt. 2.

40. Ellwood P. Cubberley, *Changing Conceptions of Education* (Boston: Houghton Mifflin, 1909), pp. 63, 56–57.

41. Ibid.; on assimilation as a central theme in twentieth-century education, see Patricia Albjerg Graham, "Assimilation, Adjustment, and Access: An Antiquarian View of American Education," in Diane Ravitch and Maris A. Vinovskis, eds., *Learning from the Past: What History Teaches Us about School Reform* (Baltimore: The Johns Hopkins University Press, 1995), pp. 3–24.

42. Ellwood P. Cubberley, "Organization of Public Education," *NEA Addresses and Proceedings, 1915,* pp. 91–97.

43. David B. Tyack, *The One Best System: A History of American Urban Education* (Cambridge: Harvard University Press, 1974), pp. 103–105.

44. Paula S. Fass, *Outside In: Minorities and the Transformation of American Education* (New York: Oxford University Press, 1989), p. 16, ch. 1; Cubberley, *Changing Conceptions;* John Dewey, *The School and Society* (Chicago: University of Chicago Press, 1899).

45. Julie A. Reuben, "Beyond Politics: Community Civics and the Redefinition of Citizenship in the Progressive Era," *History of Education Quarterly* 37 (Winter 1997): 399–420; Mary Antin, *The Promised Land* (Boston:

Houghton Mifflin, 1912); David Tyack and Michael Berkowitz, "The Man Nobody Liked: Toward a Social History of the Truant Officer, 1840–1940," *American Quarterly* 26 (Spring 1977): 321–254; Adele Marie Shaw, "The True Character of New York Public Schools," *World's Work* 7 (December 1903): 4204–4221; Julia Richman, "The Immigrant Child," *NEA Addresses and Proceedings, 1905*, pp. 113–121.

46. Sarah O'Brien, *English for Foreigners* (Boston: Houghton Mifflin, 1909), pp. 140–141, 149; in 1965 one of my students lent me a copy of O'Brien's book that had been handed down in her family from generation to generation, like a family Bible.

47. Hannah Arendt, "The Crisis in Education," *Partisan Review* 25 (1958): 493.

48. "The American Policy," *Judge,* April 20, 1901 (cover picture).

49. Thomas James, *Exile Within: The Schooling of Japanese Americans, 1942–1945* (Cambridge: Harvard University Press, 1987); Mary Bonzo Suzuki, "American Education in the Philippines, the Early Years: American Pioneer Teachers and the Filipino Response, 1900–1935" (Ph.D. diss., University of California at Berkeley, 1990); David Wallace Adams, *Education for Extinction: American Indians and the Boarding School Experience, 1875–1928* (Lawrence: University Press of Kansas, 1995); Margaret Szasz, *Education and the American Indian: The Road to Self-Determination, 1928–1973* (Albuquerque: University of New Mexico Press, 1974), ch. 1; Toshio Nishi, *Unconditional Democracy: Education and Politics in Occupied Japan, 1945–52* (Stanford: Hoover Institution Press, 1982); William D. Zeller, *An Educational Drama: The Educational Program Provided the Japanese-Americans during the Relocation Period, 1942–1945* (New York: The American Press, 1969).

50. James, *Exile;* Kenton J. Clymer, "Humanitarian Imperialism: David Prescott Barrows and the White Man's Burden in the Philippines," *Pacific Historical Review* 45 (November 1976): 495–517; James D. Clayton, *The Years of MacArthur,* vol. 1, 1880–1941 (Boston: Houghton Mifflin, 1970); Douglas MacArthur, *Reminiscences: General of the Army* (New York: McGraw Hill, 1964); Judith Raftery, "Textbook Wars: Governor-General James Francis Smith and the Protestant-Catholic Conflict in Public Education in the Phiippines, 1904–1907," *History of Education Quarterly* 38 (Summer 1998): 143–164.

51. Francis Paul Prucha, ed., *Americanizing the American Indians: Writings by the "Friends of the Indian," 1880–1900* (Cambridge: Harvard University Press, 1973); David Wallace Adams, "Fundamental Considerations: The Deep Meaning of Native American Schooling, 1880–1900," *Harvard Educational*

Review 58 (1988): 3, and passim; Brian W. Dippie, *The Vanishing American: White Attitudes and U.S. Indian Policy* (Middletown, Conn.: Wesleyan University Press, 1982), ch. 2; Robert H. Keller, Jr., *American Protestantism and United States Indian Policy* (Lincoln: University of Nebraska Press, 1983); Francis Paul Prucha, *American Indian Policy in Crisis, 1865–1900* (Norman: University of Oklahoma Press, 1976.

52. Richard H. Pratt, "The Advantages of Mingling Indians with Whites," in Prucha, ed., *Americanizing,* pp. 260–261; Commissioner of Indian Affairs quoted in David Wallace Adams, "Schooling the Hopi: Federal Indian Policy Writ Small, 1887–1917," *Pacific Historical Review* 48 (August 1979): 341; Secretary of the Interior quoted in Elaine Goodman Eastman, *Pratt: The Red Man's Moses* (Norman: University of Oklahoma Press, 1935), p. 95.

53. Richard Henry Pratt, *Battlefield and Classroom: Four Decades with the American Indian, 1867–1904,* ed. Robert M. Utley (New Haven: Yale University Press, 1954); missionary quoted by Adams, "Fundamental Considerations," p. 3.

54. T. J. Morgan, "Instructions to Indian Agents in Regard to Inculcation of Patriotism in Indian Schools," *Fifty-Ninth Annual Report of the Commissioner of Indian Affairs to the Secretary of the Interior* (Washington, D.C., 1890), p. clxvii; Morgan's comment at Hampton quoted in Adams, "Schooling the Hopi," p. 350.

55. West Virginia State Board of Education v. Barnette, 319 U.S. 624 (1943).

56. Minersville School District v. Gobitis, 310 U.S. 586 (1940).

57. Bessie Louise Pierce, *Public Opinion and the Teaching of History in the United States* (New York: Knopf, 1926), p. 18.

58. Steve Farkas and Jean Johnson, *Given the Circumstances: Teachers Talk about Public Education Today* (New York: Public Agenda, 1996), pp. 27–31, 42–43; Michael Frisch, "American History and the Structures of Collective Memory: A Modest Exercise in Empirical Iconography," *Journal of American History* 75 (1989): 1147, 1130–55; Steven Brint, Mary F. Contreras, and Michael T. Matthews, "Socialization Messages in Primary Schools: An Organizational Analysis," *Sociology of Education* 74 (July 2001): 157–180; Brint and his colleagues find that the dominant socialization ideology of the teachers they studied could be called "pluralist neo-traditionalism," a mixture of old and new values, with special attention to traits such as industry that maintain organizational stability and steady output.

59. Willard Waller, *The Sociology of Teaching* (New York: Wiley, 1965); Katherine G. Simon, *Moral Questions in the Classroom: How to Get Kids to Think*

Deeply about Real Life and Their Schoolwork (New Haven: Yale University Press, 2001); Ronald Takaki, "The Unities in Pluralism," in National Endowment for the Humanities, *A National Conversation on American Pluralism and Identity: Scholars' Essays* (Washington, D.C.: National Endowment for the Humanities, 1995), p. 31.

60. Jonathan Zimmermann, *Whose America? Culture Wars in the Public Schools* (Cambridge: Harvard University Press, 2002), p. 228.

2. Patriotic Literacy

1. Immigration and Naturalization Service, Department of Justice, *100 Typical Questions*, WR709 2211 (Washington: Government Printing Office, 1993); 2002 version available from htte://www.ins.usdoj.gov/graphics/services/natz/100g.pdf.

2. Michael Frisch, "American History and the Structures of Collective Memory: A Modest Exercise in Empirical Iconography," *Journal of American History* 75 (1989): 1147, 1130–1155.

3. *Congressional Record,* Jan. 18, 1995, S1080; Linda Symcox, "A Case Study in the Politics of Educational Reform in the U.S.: The Storm over *The National Standards for History*," *Annali di Storia Moderna e Contemporanea* 4 (1998): 493, 479–501; Gary B. Nash, Charlotte Crabtree, and Ross E. Dunn, *History on Trial: Culture Wars and the Teaching of the Past* (New York: Knopf, 1998), pp. 231–233.

4. Frances Fitzgerald, *America Revised: History Schoolbooks in the Twentieth Century* (New York: Vintage Books, 1979), p. 7.

5. David Tyack, "Monuments between Covers: The Politics of Textbooks," *American Behavioral Scientist* 42 (March 1999): 922–932; Michael Schudson, "Textbook Politics," *Journal of Communication* 44 (1994): 43–51.

6. Jonathan Zimmerman, *Whose America? Culture Wars in the Public Schools* (Cambridge: Harvard University Press, 2002).

7. Catherine Cornbleth and Dexter Waugh, *The Great Speckled Bird: Multicultural Politics and Education Policy-Making* (New York: St. Martin's Press, 1995); James W. Loewen, *Lies My Teacher Told Me: Everything Your American History Textbook Got Wrong* (New York: Touchstone Press, 1995); Michael W. Apple and Linda Christian-Smith, eds., *The Politics of the Textbook* (New York: Routledge, 1991).

8. Emma Willard, *Abbreviated History of the United States* (New York: A. S. Barnes & Co., 1852), p. vi. I examined thirty-five American history texts at the Special Collections in the Teachers College Columbia Library and

several each at four other collections. I cite many of these books here. I found the prefaces of these texts particularly useful in revealing the intent of the educators of the nineteenth century.

9. Charles A. Goodrich, *History of the United States of America; For the Use of Schools; Revised and Brought Down to the Present by William H. Seavey* (Boston: Brewer and Tileston, 1867), pp. 3–4; H. A. Guerber, *The Story of the Great Republic* (New York: American Book Co., 1899), preface.

10. Guerber, *Great Republic,* preface; C. A. Goodrich, *History of the United States,* 1828, p. 6, as quoted in William F. Russell, *The Early Teaching of History in the Secondary Schools of New York and Massachusetts* (Philadelphia: McKinley Publishing Co., 1915), p. 13.

11. Elizabeth P. Peabody, *Chronological History of the United States* (New York: Sheldon Blakeman Co., 1856), p. 7; Michael Schudson, *The Good Citizen: A History of American Civic Life* (New York: The Free Press, 1998), ch. 4.

12. The word "eclectic" appeared in the titles and prefaces of many of the textbooks, suggesting that textbooks were more collected than written.

13. Ruth Miller Elson, *Guardians of Tradition: American Textbooks of the Nineteenth Century* (Lincoln: University of Nebraska Press, 1964); Bessie L. Pierce, *Public Opinion and the Teaching of History in the United States* (New York: Knopf, 1926); Zimmerman, *Whose America?*

14. Michael V. Belok, *Forming the American Minds: Early School-Books and Their Compilers, 1783–1837* (Moti Katra, India: Satish Book Enterprise, 1973); Elson, *Guardians,* ch. 1.

15. On plagiarism in compilations see Jean H. Baker, *Affairs of Party: The Political Culture of Northern Democrats in the Mid-Nineteenth Century* (Ithaca: Cornell University Press, 1983), p. 81.

16. Pierce, *Public Opinion and the Teaching of History,* p. 29, chs. 1–2.

17. Ibid.

18. Fitzgerald, *America;* Harriet Tyson-Bernstein, *A Conspiracy of Good Intentions: America's Textbook Fiasco* (Washington, D.C.: Council for Basic Education, 1988).

19. Hillel Black, *The American Schoolbook* (New York: William Morrow & Co., 1967), pp. 132–140; Charles A. Madison, *Book Publishing in America* (New York: McGraw-Hill Book Co., 1966), pp. 122–125.

20. Edward Channing, *First Lessons in U.S. History* (New York: Macmillan Co., 1906), preface; Edward Eggleston, *A First Book in American History with Special Reference to the Lives and Deeds of Great Americans* (New York: American Book Co., 1899); Thomas Wentworth Higginson, *Young Folks' History of the United States* (Boston: Lee and Shepard, 1887).

21. C. A. Goodrich, as quoted in Russell, *Early Teaching*, p. 20; L. J. Campbell, *A Concise School History of the United States Based on Seavey's Goodrich History* (New York: J. S. Schermerhorn, 1870); for the desiccated style in a popular text, see A. S. Barnes, *A Brief History of the United States* (New York: A. S. Barnes & Co., 1886).

22. Joseph Allen, *Easy Lessons in Geography and History, Designed for the Use of the Younger Classes in the New England Schools* (Boston: Hilliard, Gray, Little, and Wilkins, 1829), p. 20; Noah Webster, *The American Spelling Book* (Boston: Isaiah Thomas and Ebenezer Andrews, 1798), pp. 145–152, 154–155.

23. John J. Anderson, *A Grammar School History of the United States* (New York: Clark & Maynard, 1874).

24. Student note in Alexander Johnson, *A History of the United States for Schools* (New York: Henry Hall & Co., 1902), inside front cover.

25. For Bunyan's *Pilgrim's Progress* as an allegory favored by Protestant educators, see David Tyack and Elisabeth Hansot, *Managers of Virtue: Public School Leadership in America, 1820–1980* (New York: Basic Books, 1982), p. 16.

26. Goodrich, *History*, pp. 227, 352.

27. As examples of two antislavery texts see Edward S. Ellis, *Young People's History of Our Country* (New York: Thomas R. Shewell & Co., 1899); Thomas Hunter, *A Narrative History of the United States for the Use of Schools* (New York: American Book Co., 1896); Hunter called slavery "a sin against God and a crime against men"; see below for pro-southern books.

28. Henry E. Chambers, *A Higher History of the United States for Schools and Academies* (New York and New Orleans: University Publishing Co., 1889), p. 357; M. E. Thalheimer, *The New Eclectic History of the United States* (New York: American Book Co., 1881); Allen C. Thomas, *A History of the United States* (Boston: D.C. Heath, 1900), p. 63.

29. William Swinton, *A Condensed School History of the United States* (New York: Ivison, Blakeman, & Co., 1871), p. iv.

30. Charles Leslie Glenn, *The Myth of the Common School* (Amherst, Mass.: University of Massachusetts Press, 1988).

31. John Gilmary Shea, *A School History of the United States, from the Earliest Period to the Present Time* (New York: Edward Dunigan and Brothers, 1858), preface, pp. 4, 9, 11, 62–64, 72, 282.

32. Chambers, *A History*, pp. 175–177, quote on 354, 357; Susan Pendleton Lee, *A School History of the United States* (Richmond, Va.: B. J. Johnson Publishing Co., 1895); I. Branson, *First Book in Composition Applying the Principles of Grammar to the Art of Composing; Also Giving Full Direction for*

Punctuation Especially Designed for the Use of Southern Schools (Raleigh: Branson, Farrar, & Co., 1863); Lee, *A School History;* Anon., *The Confederate First Reader: Containing Selections in Prose and Poetry, As Reading Exercises for the Younger Children in the Schools and Families of the Confederate States* (Richmond: G. L. Bidgood, 1864).

33. As quoted in Pierce, *History,* pp. 66–67.

34. Pierce, *Teaching of History,* p. 102, ch. 4; Zimmerman, *Whose America?* Walter Lippmann, *American Inquisitors: A Commentary on Dayton and Chicago* (New York: Macmillan, 1928); Edmund Hartmann, *The Movement to Americanize the Immigrant* (New York: Columbia University Press, 1948).

35. Lippmann, *American Inquisitors;* historian as quoted in Fitzgerald, *America,* p. 35.

36. Bessie Louise Pierce, *Citizens' Organizations and the Civic Training of Youth* (New York: Charles Scribner's Sons, 1933); Jonathan Zimmerman, "Storm over the Schoolhouse: Exploring Popular Influences upon the American Curriculum, 1890–1941," *Teachers College Record* 100 (Spring 1999): 602–626.

37. Micheline Fedyck, "Conceptions of Citizenship and Nationality in High School American History Textbooks, 1913–1977" (Ph.D. diss., Columbia University, 1980), pp. 109, 101–114.

38. Text quoted in Bessie Louise Pierce, *Civic Attitudes in American School Textbooks* (Chicago: University of Chicago Press, 1930), pp. 87–88.

39. Fedyck, "Conceptions of Citizenship," pp. 110–114.

40. Mary Antin, *The Promised Land* (Boston: Houghton Mifflin, 1912), p. 223; Jacob Riis, *The Children of the Poor* (New York: Charles Scribner's Sons, 1892), pp. 53–54.

41. Louis Adamic, *From Many Lands* (New York: Harper & Brothers, 1939), pp. 243–244.

42. Zimmerman, *Whose America?* pp. 65–80; Herbert M. Kliebard and Greg Wegner, "Harold Rugg and the Reconstruction of the Social Studies Curriculum: The Treatment of the 'Great War' in His Textbook Series," in Thomas S. Popkewitz, ed., *The Formation of School Subjects: The Struggle for Creating an American Institution* (New York: Falmer Press, 1987), pp. 268–287; the Rugg papers in the Teachers College archives give rich documentation on Rugg's battles.

43. Zimmerman, *Whose America?* and personal communication to David Tyack, Sept. 4, 2002.

44. Gary B. Nash, "American History Reconsidered: Asking New Questions about the Past," in Diane Ravitch and Maris A. Vinovskis, eds., *Learning*

from the Past: What History Teaches Us about School Reform (Baltimore: The Johns Hopkins University Press, 1995), pp. 135–163.

45. Jean Anyon, "Ideology and United States History Textbooks," *Harvard Educational Review* 49 (August 1979): 361–386; Christine E. Sleeter and Carl A. Grant, "An Analysis of Multicultural Education in the United States," *Harvard Educational Review* 57 (November 1987): 421–444; Mary Kay Tetrault, "Thinking about Women: The Case of United States History Textbooks," *History Teacher* 19 (1986): 211–262.

46. Nathan Glazer and Reed Ueda, *Ethnicity in History Textbooks* (Washington, D.C.: Ethics and Public Policy Center, 1983); Anyon, "Ideology"; Tetrault, "Thinking about Women."

47. Feiffer quoted by Nash, "American History Reconsidered," p. 144; for studies of blue-collar and white ethnic patriotism, see John Bodnar, ed., *Bonds of Affection: Americans Define Their Patriotism* (Princeton: Princeton University Press, 1996), and Bodnar, *Remaking America: Public Memory, Commemoration, and Patriotism in the Twentieth Century* (Princeton: Princeton University Press, 1992).

48. Nash, Crabtree, and Dunn, *History on Trial;* Tyack, "Monuments between Covers," pp. 922–932.

49. Cornbleth and Waugh, *Speckled Bird,* p. 79; Richard Rothstein, "In Schoolbooks, History Often Gets a Lift and a Tuck," *New York Times,* Oct. 2, 2002, p. A23.

50. Harriet Tyson-Bernstein, *A Conspiracy of Good Intentions: America's Textbook Fiasco* (Washington, D.C.: Council for Basic Education, 1988).

51. Loewen, *Lies My Teacher Told Me,* p. 279.

52. A. Stille describes a happy exception, a brilliant textbook, in "The Betrayal of History," *New York Review of Books,* June 11, 1998, pp. 15–20.

53. Greg Winter, "More Schools Rely on Tests, But Big Study Raises Doubts," *New York Times,* Dec. 28, 2002, pp. A1, A13.

54. Loewen, *Lies My Teacher Told Me,* pp. 286–288.

55. Joan Delfattore, *What Johnny Shouldn't Read: Textbook Censorship in America* (New Haven: Yale University Press, 1992); Tyson-Bernstein, *Conspiracy;* Stille, "Betrayal."

56. Patricia Nelson Limerick, "The Battlefield of History," *New York Times,* July 28, 1997, p. A19.

57. Katherine G. Simon, *Moral Questions in the Classroom: How to Get Kids to Think Deeply about Real Life and Their Schoolwork* (New Haven: Yale University Press, 2001).

3. Same or Different?

1. Marilyn Halter, *Between Race and Ethnicity: Cape Verdean American Immigrants, 1860–1965* (Urbana and Chicago: University of Illinois Press, 1993), p. 146 on the 250 phenotypical categories; David Tyack, "Cape Verdean Immigration to the United States," (B.A. thesis, Harvard University, 1952).

2. Arthur Mann, *The One and the Many: Reflections on the American Identity* (Chicago: University of Chicago Press, 1979); Gunnar Myrdal, *An American Dilemma: The Negro Problem and Modern Democracy* (New York: Harper & Bros., 1944).

3. Robert K. Fullinwider, ed., *Public Education in a Multicultural Society: Policy, Theory, Critique* (Cambridge: Cambridge University Press, 1996); Lawrence A. Cremin, *Popular Education and Its Discontents* (New York: Harper & Row, 1990), pp. 85–125; Molefi Kete Asante, *The Afrocentric Idea* (Philadelphia: Temple University Press, 1987); Paul Gray, "Whose America?" *Time,* July 8, 1991, pp. 13–17; Karen De Witt, "Rise Is Forecast in Minorities in the Schools," *New York Times,* Sept. 13, 1991, p. A8; Jane Gross, "A City's Determination to Rewrite History Puts Its Classrooms in Chaos," *New York Times,* Sept. 18, 1991, p. B7 (on Oakland, California, see also Gary Yee, "Values in Conflict," unpublished study of ethnic conflict over curriculum, Stanford University, June 10, 1991); Eleanor Armour-Thomas and William A. Proefriedt, "Cultural Interdependence and 'Learner-Centrism,'" *Education Week,* Dec. 4, 1991, pp. 36, 27.

4. On constitutional issues, see David L. Kirp and Mark G. Yudof, *Educational Policy and the Law: Cases and Materials* (Berkeley: McCutchan, 1974); on obfuscations in dealing with class, see Benjamin DeMott, *The Imperial Middle: Why Americans Can't Think Straight about Class* (New York: William Morrow and Co., 1990), and Richard Rubinson, "Class Formation, Politics, and Institutions: Schooling in the United States," *American Journal of Sociology* 92 (November 1986): 519–548.

5. Michael B. Katz, *The Undeserving Poor: From the War on Poverty to the War on Welfare* (New York: Pantheon Books, 1989), pp. 5–6; Minow quoted in Katz, *Poor,* p. 167; Renato Rosaldo, "Others of Invention: Ethnicity and Its Discontents," *Village Voice Literary Supplement,* February 1990, no. 82, pp. 27–29.

6. Horace Mann Bond, "Main Currents in the Educational Crisis Affecting Afro-Americans," *Freedomways* 8 (Fall 1968): 308; on the Nazi incident—which upset some whites who normally took caste for granted—see Mor-

ton Sosna, "Stalag Dixie," *Stanford Humanities Review* 2 (Spring 1990): 38–64; Barbara Jeanne Fields, "Slavery, Race, and Ideology in the United States of America," *New Left Review* 181 (May-June 1990): 95–119.

7. Clifford Geertz, *Local Knowledge* (New York: Basic Books, 1983), pp. 80–84.

8. Tessie Liu, "Teaching the Differences among Women from a Historical Perspective: Rethinking Race and Gender as Social Categories," *Women Studies International Forum* 14, no. 4 (1990): 265–276.

9. Joel Perlmann, *Ethnic Difference* (Cambridge: Cambridge University Press, 1988); Nicholas V. Montalto, *A History of the Intercultural Educational Movement, 1924–1941* (New York: Garland Publishing Co., 1982); Stephan F. Brumberg, *Going to America, Going to School: The Jewish Immigrant Public School Encounter in Turn-of-the-Century New York City* (New York: Praeger, 1986); Renato Rosaldo, "Assimilation Revisited," in *In Times of Challenge: Chicanos and Chicanas in American Society* Mexican American Studies Monograph Series no. 6 (Houston: University of Houston, 1988), pp. 43–49; Gary Gerstle, *Working-Class Americanism: The Politics of Labor in a Textile City, 1914–1960* (New York: Cambridge University Press, 1989); John Bodnar, *The Transplanted: A History of Immigrants in Urban America* (Bloomington: Indiana University Press, 1985); David A. Hollinger, *Postethnic America: Beyond Multiculturalism* (New York: Basic Books, 1995).

10. Henry Louis Gates, Jr., commencement address at Emory University, May 8, 1995, cited in *Emory Report,* May 15, 1995.

11. David Tyack, "Pilgrim's Progress: Toward a Social History of the School Superintendency," *History of Education Quarterly* 16 (1976): 295–300; Paula Fass, *Outside In: Minorities and the Transformation of American Education* (New York: Oxford University Press, 1989); Paul Peterson, *The Politics of School Reform, 1870–1940* (Chicago: University of Chicago Press, 1985).

12. *Addresses and Proceedings of the NEA,* 1891, pp. 395, 398, 393–403.

13. George T. Balch, *Methods of Teaching Patriotism in the Public Schools* (New York: D. Van Nostrand Co., 1890). John Higham, *Strangers in the Land: Patterns of American Nativism* (New York: Athenaeum, 1966); Oscar Handlin, *Race and Nationality in American Life* (Boston: Little, Brown, 1957).

14. U.S. Immigration Commission, *Children of Immigrants in Schools* (Washington, D.C.: Government Printing Office, 1911), vol. 1, pp. 14–15; David Tyack and Michael Berkowitz,"The Man Nobody Liked: Toward a Social History of the Truant Officer, 1840–1940," *American Quarterly,* 26 (Spring 1977): 321–354; Ellwood P. Cubberley, *Changing Conceptions of Education* (Boston: Houghton Mifflin, 1909), pp. 63–64; Adele Marie Shaw, "The

True Character of New York Public Schools," *World's Work* 7 (December 1903): 4204–4221; Michael Olneck, "Americanization and the Education of Immigrants, 1900–1925: An Analysis of Symbolic Action," *American Journal of Education* 98 (August 1989): 398, 398–423.

15. Helen M. Todd, "Why Children Work: The Children's Answer," *McClure's Magazine* 40 (April 1913): 68–79; William H. Dooley, *The Education of the Ne'er-Do-Well* (Boston: Houghton Mifflin, 1916); Robert A. Carlson, *The Americanization Syndrome: A Quest for Conformity* (London: Croom Helm, 1987); Leonard Covello, "A High School and Its Immigrant Community—a Challenge and an Opportunity," *Journal of Educational Sociology* 9 (February 1936): 331–346; Peter Roberts, *The Problem of Americanization* (New York: Macmillan, 1920).

16. William J. Reese, *Power and the Promise of School Reform: Grass-Roots Movements during the Progressive Era* (Boston: Routledge & Kegan Paul, 1986), p. 231.

17. Edward G. Hartmann, *The Movement to Americanize the Immigrant* (New York: Columbia University Press, 1948).

18. John Dewey, "Nationalizing Education," *NEA Addresses and Proceedings, 1916*, pp. 185, 183–189; John F. McClymer, "The Americanization Movement and the Education of the Foreign-Born Adult, 1914–25," in Bernard J. Weiss, ed., *American Education and the European Immigrant: 1840–1940* (Urbana: University of Illinois Press, 1982), pp. 97, 96–116.

19. Jesse K. Flanders, *Legislative Control of the Elementary Curriculum* (New York: Teachers College, 1925), pp. 62; David Tyack, Thomas James, and Aaron Benavot, *Law and the Shaping of Public Education, 1785–1954* (Madison: University of Wisconsin Press, 1987), chs. 6–7.

20. Stephan F. Brumberg, "New York City Schools March Off to War: The Nature and Extent of Participation of the City Schools in the Great War, April 1917–June 1918," *Urban Education* 24 (January 1990): 440–475; McClymer, "Americanization."

21. Horace M. Kallen, *Culture and Democracy in the United States: Studies in the Group Psychology of the American Peoples* (New York: Boni and Liveright, 1924), pp. 139, 122, 124, 121–124; for a critique of Kallen's proposals, including his racist attitudes toward African-Americans, see Werner Sollors, "A Critique of Pure Pluralism," in Sacvan Berkovitch, ed., *Reconstructing American Literacy History* (Cambridge: Harvard University Press, 1986), pp. 250–279.

22. Todd, "Why Children Work"; Bodnar, *Transplanted;* Timothy L. Smith, "Immigrant Social Aspirations and American Education, 1880–1930," *Ameri-*

can Quarterly 21 (Fall 1969): 523–543; David K. Cohen, "Immigrants and the Schools," *Review of Educational Research* 70 (February 1970): 13–26; Weiss, ed., *Immigrant;* Jonathan Zimmerman, "Ethnics against Ethnicity: European Immigrants and Foreign-Language Instruction, 1890–1940," *Journal of American History* 88 (March 2002): 1383–1404.

23. Nicholas V. Montalto, "The Intercultural Education Movement, 1924–41: The Growth of Tolerance as a Form of Intolerance," in Weiss, ed., *Immigrant,* pp. 144, 142–160; John Daniels, *America via the Neighborhood* (New York: Harper & Brothers, 1920).

24. Albert Shiels, "Education for Citizenship," *NEA Addresses and Proceedings, 1922,* pp. 934–940; Marcus E. Ravage, "The Immigrant's Burden," *The New Republic* 19 (June 1919): 209–211; Daniel E. Weinberg, "The Ethnic Technician and the Foreign-Born: Another Look at Americanization Ideology and Goals," *Societas* 7 (Summer 1977): 209–227; William C. Smith, *Americans in the Making* (New York: D. Appleton-Century, 1939); Ronald D. Cohen, *Children of the Mill: Schooling and Society in Gary, Indiana, 1906–1960* (Bloomington: Indiana University Press, 1990); Montalto, *Movement,* chs. 1–2.

25. Department of Supervisors and Directors of Instruction, NEA, *Americans All: Studies in Intercultural Education* (Washington, D.C.: NEA, 1942).

26. Montalto, "Movement"; Rachel Davis DuBois, "Our Enemy—the Stereotype," *Progressive Education* 12 (March 1935): 146–150.

27. Louis Adamic, "Thirty Million New Americans," *Harpers Monthly Magazine* 169 (November 1934): 684–694; Park quoted in Montalto, *Movement,* p. 22; Robert Schaffer, "Multicultural Education in New York City during World War II," *New York History* (July 1996): 301–332.

28. Montalto, "Movement," p. 147.

29. Critic and superintendents quoted in Montalto, *Movement,* p. 249; for a critique of the shallowness and patchy character of some "intergroup" curriculums, see Theodore Brameld, "Intergroup Education in Certain School Systems," *Harvard Educational Review* 15 (March 1945): 93–98, and Ronald K. Goodenough, "The Progressive Educator, Race, and Ethnicity in the Depression Years: An Overview," *History of Education Quarterly* 15 (Winter 1975): 365–394.

30. Olneck, "Symbolism and Ideology," pp. 147–174; Julie A. Reuben, "Beyond Politics: Community Civics and the Redefinition of Citizenship in the Progressive Era," *History of Education Quarterly* 37 (Winter 1997): 399–420.

31. Carol D. Lee, Kofi Lomotey, and Mwalimu Shujaa, "How Shall We Sing our Sacred Song in a Strange Land? The Dilemma of Double Conscious-

ness and the Complexities of an African-centered Pedagogy," *Journal of Education* 172, no. 2 (1990): 45–61; Christine E. Sleeter and Carl A. Grant, "An Analysis of Multicultural Education in the United States," *Harvard Educational Review* 57 (November 1987): 421–444; James Banks, *Teaching Strategies for Ethnic Studies* (Boston: Allyn and Bacon, 1991); for a study of types of multicultural education in Australia, see Fazal Rizvi, *Ethnicity, Class, and Multicultural Education* (Deakin, Victoria: Deakin University Press, 1986).

32. Joyce Elaine King and Gloria Ladson-Billings, "Dysconscious Racism and Multicultural Illiteracy: The Distorting of the American Mind," paper presented at the annual meeting of the American Educational Research Association, April 16–20, 1991, Boston; Gross, "Classrooms in Chaos," p. B7; Laurie Olsen, *Crossing the Schoolhouse Border: Immigrant Students and the California Public Schools* (San Francisco: California Tomorrow, 1988); David L. Kirp, "Textbooks and Tribalism in California," *The Public Interest* 104 (Summer 1991): 20–36; Diane Ravitch, "Diversity and Democracy: Multicultural Education in America," *American Educator* 14 (Spring 1990): 16–20, 46–48.

33. James D. Anderson, *The Education of Blacks in the South, 1860–1935* (Chapel Hill: University of North Carolina Press, 1988); W. E. B. Du Bois, *The Negro Common School* (Atlanta: Atlanta University Press, 1901); Louis R. Harlan, *Separate and Unequal: Public Schools and Racism in the Southern Seaboard States* (New York: Athenaeum, 1968).

34. Ronald Takaki, *Strangers from a Different Shore: A History of Asian Americans* (New York: Penguin Books, 1989); Thomas James, *Exiles Within: The Schooling of Japanese Americans, 1942–1945* (Cambridge: Harvard University Press, 1987); Elliott Grinnell Mears, *Resident Orientals on the Pacific Coast: Their Legal and Economic Status* (Chicago: University of Chicago Press, 1928).

35. Meyer Weinberg, *A Chance to Learn: A History of Race and Education in the United States* (New York: Cambridge University Press, 1977), pp. 165–166; Guadalupe San Miguel, *"Let Them All Take Heed": Mexican Americans and the Campaign for Educational Equality in Texas, 1910–1981* (Austin: University of Texas Press, 1987); Albert Camarillo, *Chicanos in a Changing Society* (Cambridge: Harvard University Press, 1984).

36. Superintendent quoted in Weinberg, *Chance to Learn*, p. 146; Ruben Donato, *The Other Struggle for Equal Schools: Mexican Americans during the Civil Rights Era* (Albany: State University of New York Press, 1997).

37. Fields, "Race"; Horace Mann Bond, *The Education of the Negro in the American Social Order* (1934; reprint, New York: Octagon Books, 1966);

Richard Wright, *12,000,000 Black Voices* (New York: Viking, 1941); George M. Frederickson, *The Arrogance of Race: Historical Perspectives on Slavery, Racism, and Social Inequality* (Middletown, Conn.: Wesleyan University Press, 1988).

38. Rolland Dewing, "Teacher Organizations and Desegregation," *Phi Delta Kappan* 49 (January 1968): 257–260.

39. Bond, *Education of the Negro,* chs. 15–16; Doxey A. Wilkerson, "A Determination of the Peculiar Problems of Negroes in Contemporary American Society," *Journal of Negro Education* 5 (July 1936): 324–350; W. E. B. Du Bois, *The Philadelphia Negro* (Philadelphia: University Press, 1899); William L. Buckley, "The Industrial Condition of the Negro in New York city," *Annals of the American Academy of Political and Social Science* 27 (May 1906): 590–596; for a study of the persistence of black faith in schooling, however, see Timothy Smith, "Native Blacks and Foreign Whites: Varying Responses to Educational Opportunity in America, 1890–1950," *Perspectives in American History* 6 (1972): 309–335.

40. Goodenough, "Progressive Educator."

41. W. E. B. Du Bois, "Pechstein and Pecksniff," *The Crisis* 36 (September 1929): 313–314; Du Bois, "Does the Negro Need Separate Schools?" *Journal of Negro Education* 4 (July 1935): 328–335.

42. Bond, *Education of the Negro,* preface; Paula Fass, *Outside In: Minorities and the Transformation of American Education* (New York: Oxford University Press, 1989), ch. 4; David Tyack, Robert Lowe, and Elisabeth Hansot, *Public Schools in Hard Times: The Great Depression and Recent Years* (Cambridge: Harvard University Press, 1984), pp. 122, 125, 126, 182, 196.

43. Fass, *Outside In,* ch. 4.

44. W. E. B. Du Bois, "Two Hundred Years of Segregated Schools," in Philip S. Foner, ed., *W. E. B. Du Bois Speaks: Speeches and Addresses, 1920–1963* (New York: Pathfinder Press, 1970), p. 238; Weinberg, *Chance to Learn,* ch. 3; Richard Kluger, *Simple Justice: The History of Brown v. Board of Education and Black America's Struggle for Equality* (New York: Vintage Books, 1977).

45. J. Harvie Wilkerson III, *From Brown to Bakke: The Supreme Court and School Integration, 1954–1978* (New York: Random House, 1979).

46. Weinberg, *Chance to Learn,* pp. 122–124, 131; Dorothy Jones, "The Issues at I.S. 201: A View from the Parents' Committee," in Meyer Weinberg, ed., *Integrated Education: A Reader* (Beverly Hills: The Glencoe Press, 1968), pp. 155–157; Robert C. Maynard, "Black Nationalism and Community Schools," in Henry Levin, ed., *Community Control of Schools* (Washington, D.C.: The Brookings Institution, 1970), pp. 100–101.

47. Robert Newby and David Tyack, "Victims without 'Crimes': Some Historical Perspectives on Black Education," *Journal of Negro Education* 40 (Summer 1971): 192–206; I am very grateful to Bob Newby for the illuminating conversations we had about these matters some thirty years ago.

48. Du Bois, "Segregated Schools," p. 238; A. Wade Boykin, "The Triple Quandary and the Schooling of Afro-American Children," and John U. Ogbu, "Variability in Minority Responses to Schooling: Nonimmigrants v. Immigrants," in Ulric Neisser, ed., *The School Achievement of Minority Children* (Hillsdale, N.J.: Lawrence Erlbaum Associates, 1986), pp. 57–92, 255–278; Joyce Elaine King and Thomasyne Lightfoote Wilson, "Being the Soul-Freeing Substance: A Legacy of Hope in Afro Humanity," *Journal of Education* 172, no. 2 (1990): 9–27; Molefi Kete Asante, "The Afrocentric Idea in Education," *Journal of Negro Education* 60 (Spring 1991): 170–180.

49. Nancy Frazier and Myra Sadker, *Sexism in School and Society* (New York: Harper & Row, 1973), p. 2; many women active in civil rights protested what they saw as discrimination against females in the movement.

50. William Chafe, *Women and Equality: Changing Patterns in American Culture* (New York: Oxford University Press, 1977), ch. 3; E. R. Feagin and Clairese Booher Feagin, *Discrimination American Style: Institutional Racism and Sexism* (Englewood Cliffs, N.J.: Prentice-Hall, 1978); David Tyack and Elisabeth Hansot, *Learning Together: A History of Coeducation in American Schools* (New Haven: Yale University Press and The Russell Sage Foundation, 1990), chs. 2–3.

51. Horace Mann, *A Few Thoughts on the Powers and Duties of Women* (Syracuse: Hall, Mills, and Co., 1853), p. 57; Tyack and Hansot, *Learning Together,* chs. 2–3.

52. Tyack and Hansot, *Learning Together,* chs. 8–9.

53. For analysis of conservative opposition by both sexes to the feminist agenda, see Theresa Cusick, *A Clash of Ideologies: The Reagan Administration versus the Women's Educational Equity Act* (Washington, D.C.: PEER, 1983).

54. William D. Lewis, "The High School and the Boy," *The Saturday Evening Post* 184 (April 6, 1912): 8–9, 77–78; Thomas Woody, *A History of Women's Education in the United States,* 2 vols. (New York: Science Press, 1929).

55. Emma Willard, *A Plan for Improving Female Education* (1819; reprint, Middlebury, Vt.: Middlebury College, 1919); Edward D. Mansfield, *American Education: Its Principles and Elements, Dedicated to the Teachers of the United States* (New York: A. S. Barnes, 1851), ch. 14.

56. Leta S. Hollingsworth, "Comparison of the Sexes in Mental Traits," *The Psychological Bulletin* 15 (1918): 428; Rosalind Rosenberg, *Beyond Separate Spheres: Intellectual Roots of Modern Feminism* (New Haven: Yale University Press, 1982).

57. Feagin and Feagin, *Discrimination American Style,* chs. 1–2, 5; Janice Pottker and Andrew Fishel, eds., *Sex Bias in the Schools: The Research Evidence* (Rutherford, N.J.: Farleigh Dickinson University Press, 1977); Susan S. Klein, ed., *Handbook for Achieving Sex Equity through Education* (Baltimore: The Johns Hopkins University Press, 1985).

58. Margaret B. Sutherland, "Whatever Happened to Coeducation?" *British Journal of Educational Studies* 33 (1986): 156–157; Carol Gilligan, *In a Different Voice: Psychological Theory and Women's Development* (Cambridge: Harvard University Press, 1982); Madeline Arnot, "A Cloud over Coeducation: An Analysis of the Forms of Transmission of Class and Gender Relations," in Stephen Walker and Len Barton, eds., *Gender, Class, and Education* (New York: Falmer Press, 1983), pp. 69–92.

59. Jane Roland Martin, *Reclaiming a Conversation: The Ideal of the Educated Woman* (New Haven: Yale University Press, 1985), p. 195.

60. John Higham, "Integration v. Pluralism: Another American Dilemma," *Center Magazine* 7 (August 1974): 68. 71 speaks of pluralist integration; Sollars, "Pluralism," p. 156–158, notes that ethnic groups are neither static nor homogeneous; Renato Rosaldo, "Assimilation," notes that it was not necessary to be culturally assimilated to get ahead economically; Tyack and Hansot, *Learning Together,* ch. 9 and conclusion.

4. Thoroughly Trained in Failure

1. Helen Todd, "Why Children Work: The Children's Answer," *McClure's Magazine* 40 (April 1913): 68–79, 73–75.

2. Ibid., 74.

3. Ibid., pp. 74, 76, 68–79.

4. Todd, "Children," pp. 73–78; Edith Waterfall, *The Day Continuation School in England: Its Function and Future* (London: George Allen and Unwin, 1923), pp. 154–155.

5. Children's Defense Fund, *Children Out of School in America* (Cambridge: Children's Defense Fund, 1974), pp. 3–4.

6. For recent studies of how schools produce failure and resistance, see Raymond P. McDermott, "Achieving School Failure 1972–1997," in George D. Spindler, ed., *Education and Cultural Process: Anthropological Approaches* (Prospect Heights, Ill.: Waveland Press, 1997); Herve Varenne and Ray

McDermott, *Successful Failure: The School America Builds* (Boulder: Westview Press, 1998); William Glasser, *Schools without Failure* (New York: Harper & Row, 1969); Henry A. Giroux, *Theory and Resistance in Education* (South Hadley, Mass.: Bergin and Garvey, 1983); Sherman Dorn, *Creating the Dropout: An Institutional and Social History of School Failure* (Westport, Conn.: Praeger, 1996).

7. Stanley J. Zehm, "Educational Misfits: A Study of Poor Performers in the English Class, 1825–1925," (Ph.D. diss., Stanford University, 1973); in my thinking about labels of students and what they might mean I am much indebted to Stan Zehm's thesis and to conversations with him over the years. This chapter is partially adapted from an essay written by Sarah Deschenes, Larry Cuban, and me, "Mismatch: Historical Perspectives on Schools and Students Who Don't Fit Them," *Teachers College Record* 103 (August 1999): 525–547.

8. Zehm, "Educational Misfits"; William Reese, *Power and the Promise of School Reform: Grass-Roots Movements during the Progressive Era* (Boston: Routledge & Kegan Paul, 1986).

9. Workingmen quoted in John Commons, ed., *American Industrial Society* (Cleveland: Arthur H. Clark Co., 1910), vol. 5, pp. 114, 116.

10. Carl F. Kaestle, *Pillars of the Republic: Common Schools and American Society, 1780–1860* (New York: Hill and Wang, 1983); Lawrence A. Cremin, *The American Common School: An Historic Conception* (New York: Bureau of Publications, Teachers College, Columbia, 1951).

11. Alvin Johnson, *Pioneer's Progress, An Autobiography* (New York: Viking Press, 1952), p. 104; David Tyack and Elisabeth Hansot, *Learning Together: A History of Coeducation in American Public Schools* (New Haven: Yale University Press and Russell Sage Foundation, 1990), ch. 3.

12. Zehm, "Educational Misfits," appendix A.

13. Warren Burton, *The District School As It Was: By One Who Went to It* (Boston: Carter, Hendee, and Co., 1833), p. 14.

14. Wayne Edison Fuller, *The Old Country School: The Story of Rural Education in the Middle West* (Chicago: University of Chicago Press, 1982); Andrew Gulliford, *America's Country Schools* (Washington, D.C.: Preservation Press, 1986.

15. As quoted from the *Brooklyn Daily Eagle,* April 13, 1846, in Florence Bernstein Freedman, *Walt Whitman Looks at the Schools* (New York: King's Crown Press, 1950), p. 102.

16. U.S. Commissioner of Education, "Classification and Promotion of Pupils," *Report for 1898–99,* pp. 303–356; David Angus, Jeffrey Mirel, and Maris Vinovskis, "Historical Development of Age Stratification in Schooling,"

Teachers College Record 90 (Winter 1988): 211–236; David B. Tyack, *The One Best System: A History of American Urban Education* (Cambridge: Harvard University Press, 1974), pt. II.

17. William Reese, *The Origins of the American High School* (New Haven: Yale University Press, 1995); David F. Labaree, *The Making of an American High School: The Credentials Market and the Central High School of Philadelphia, 1838–1939* (New Haven: Yale University Press, 1988).

18. Buffalo Public Schools, Annual Report of the Superintendent of Public Instruction, 1873, pp. 10–12; Tyack, *One Best System*, p. 71.

19. Zehm, "Educational Misfits," appendix A; Barbara Jean Finkelstein, "Governing the Young: Teacher Behavior in American Primary Schools, 1820–1880: A Documentary History" (Ph.D. diss., Teachers College, Columbia University, 1970), pp. 134–135.

20. John B. Peaslee, *Thoughts and Experiences In and Out of School* (Cincinnati: Curts and Jennings, 1899), p. 253.

21. Annual Report of the Board of Education, Cleveland, 1894, p. 70.

22. Leonard Ayres, *Laggards in Our Schools: A Study of Retardation and Elimination in City School Systems* (New York: Survey Associates, 1909), p. 3.

23. Ibid., pp. 14, 72, 88.

24. Detroit Public School Staff, *Frank Cody: A Realist in Education* (New York: Macmillan, 1943), p. 265. Joel Perlmann points out that the transformation of urban high schools was a gradual process—"Curriculum and Tracking in the Transformation of the American High School: Providence, R.I. 1880–1930," *Journal of Social History* 19 (Fall 1983): 29–55.

25. Horace Mann Bond, *The Education of the Negro in the American Social Order* (New York: Prentice-Hall, 1934).

26. Robert Hunter, *Poverty* (New York: Harper & Row, 1905), p. 209; William Wirt, "Ways and Means for a Closer Union between the School and the Non-School Activities," NEA, *Addresses and Proceedings*, 1923, p. 46; see also Thomas Eliot, "Should Courts Do Case Work?" *The Survey* 60 (September 15, 1928): 601–603.

27. Leonard Covello, *The Heart Is the Teacher* (New York: McGraw Hill, 1958), p. 124.

28. Michael Sedlak and Robert Church, *A History of Social Services Delivered to Youth, 1880–1977* (Final Report to the National Institute of Education) (Washington, D.C.: National Institute of Education, 1982); Michael W. Sedlak, "Attitudes, Choices, and Behavior: School Delivery of Health and Social Services," in Diane Ravitch and Maris Vinovskis, eds., *Learning from the Past: What History Teaches Us about School Reform* (Baltimore: The Johns

Hopkins University Press, 1995), pp. 57–94; David Tyack, "Health and Social Services in Public Schools: Historical Perspectives," *The Future of Children* 2 (1992): 19–31; Tyack, "The High School as a Service Agency: Historical Perspectives on Current Policy Issues," *Educational Evaluation and Policy Analysis* 1 (1979): 45–57.

29. Reese, *Power,* p. 225.

30. Sol Cohen, *Progressives and Urban School Reform: The Public Education Association of New York City, 1895–1954* (New York: Teachers College Press, 1964); Murray Levine and Adeline Levine, *A Social History of the Helping Services* (New York: Appleton-Century-Crofts, 1970).

31. Reese, *Power,* p. 218; Robert J. Taggart, *Private Philanthropy and Public Education: Pierre S. DuPont and the Delaware Schools, 1890–1940* (Newark: University of Delaware Press, 1988), pp. 67–70.

32. Michael Sedlak and Stephen Schlossman, "The Public School and Social Services: Reassessing the Progressive Legacy," *Educational Theory* 35 (Fall 1985): 371–383; Reese, *Power,* pp. 162–163.

33. Diane Claire Wood, "Immigrant Mothers, Female Reformers, and Women Teachers: The California Home Teacher Act of 1915" (Ph.D. diss., Stanford University, 1996); Levine and Levine, *Social History;* for the change in functions and attitudes of school social workers as they became incorporated into the bureaucratic structure of schools, see L. A. Costain, "A Historical View of School Social Work," *Social Casework* 50 (October 1969): 441, 442, 444, 439–453.

34. Stephen Schlossman, JoAnne Brown, and Michael Sedlak, *The Public School in American Dentistry* (Santa Monica, Cal.: Rand Corporation, 1986); Lawrence A. Cremin, *The Transformation of the School* (New York: Knopf, 1961).

35. Reese, *Power,* p. 225.

36. J. Rogers, *Health Services in City Schools* (Washington, D.C.: Government Printing Office, 1942); Louis Terman, *The Hygiene of the School Child* (Boston: Houghton Mifflin, 1929), p. 211, ch.1; Taggart, *Private Philanthropy,* pp. 67–70; David Tyack and Michael Berkowitz, "The Man Nobody Liked: Toward a Social History of the Truant Officer, 1840–1940," *American Quarterly* 26 (Spring 1977): 321–354; Joel Spring, *Education and the Rise of the Corporate State* (Boston: Beacon Press, 1972).

37. David Alexander Gamson, "District by Design: Progressive Education Reform in Four Western Cities" (Ph.D. diss., Stanford University, 2001).

38. Jonathan Zimmerman, *Whose America? Culture Wars in the Public Schools* (Cambridge: Harvard University Press, 2002); David Tyack, Thomas

James, and Aaron Benavot, *Law and the Shaping of Public Education, 1785–1954* (Madison: University of Wisconsin Press, 1987), ch. 6.

39. Jesse K. Flanders, *Legislative Control of the Elementary Curriculum* (New York: Teachers College Press, 1925); Bessie Pierce, *Public Opinion and the Teaching of History in the United States* (New York: Knopf, 1926); Zimmermann, *Whose America?*

40. David L. Angus and Jeffrey E. Mirel, *The Failed Promise of the American High School* (New York: Teachers College Press, 1999); Diane Ravitch, *Left Back: A Century of Failed School Reforms* (New York: Simon & Schuster, 2000); Arthur Powell, Eleanor Farrar, and David K. Cohen, *The Shopping Mall High Schools: Winners and Losers in the Educational Marketplace* (Boston: Houghton Mifflin, 1985).

41. Herbert M. Kliebard, *Schooled to Work: Vocationalism and the American Curriculum, 1876–1946* (New York: Teachers College Press, 1999).

42. Margaret M. Alltucker, "What Can the Secondary School Do for the Student of Low I.Q.?" *The School Review* 31 (1923): 656, 661, 653–661.

43. Gamson, "District by Design," pp. 162–165; Jeannie Oakes, *Keeping Track: How Schools Structure Inequality* (New Haven: Yale University Press, 1985).

44. On Baltimore, see Ellwood P. Cubberley, *Public Education in the United States* (Boston: Houghton Mifflin, 1919), p. 525; Lewis Terman, *Intelligence Tests and School Reorganization* (Yonkers-on-Hudson: World Book, 1922); Paula Fass, *Outside In: Minorities and the Transformation of American Education* (New York: Oxford University Press, 1989); Clarence J. Karier, Paul Violas, and Joel Spring, *Roots of Crisis: American Education in the Twentieth Century* (Chicago: Rand McNally, 1973).

45. Terman, *Tests;* Zehm, "Educational Misfits," appendix A.

46. E. L. Thorndike, "The University and Vocational Guidance," in Meyer Bloomfield, ed., *Readings in Vocational Guidance* (Boston: Houghton Mifflin, 1915), p. 100; Spring, *Education and Corporate State.*

47. David B. Corson, "Classification of Pupils," *Journal of Educational Administration and Supervision* 6 (September 1920): 86; Paul Davis Chapman, *Schools as Sorters: Lewis M. Terman, Applied Psychology, and the Intelligence Testing Movement, 1890–1930* (New York: New York University Press, 1988); Fass, *Inside Out.*

48. Detroit Public School Staff, *Frank Cody,* p. 265.

49. Federation quoted in Tyack, *One Best System,* p. 215.

50. Richard Kluger, *Simple Justice: The History of Brown v. Board of Education and Black America's Struggle for Equality* (New York: Knopf, 1977); Guadalupe San Miguel, Jr., *"Let All of Them Take Heed": Mexican Americans and the*

Campaign for Educational Equality in Texas, 1910–1981 (Austin: University of Texas Press, 1987).

51. William Ryan, *Blaming the Victim* (New York: Pantheon Books, 1971); David Tyack and Elisabeth Hansot, *Managers of Virtue: Public School Leadership in America, 1820–1980* (New York: Basic Books, 1982), pt. 3; Ruben Donato, *The Other Struggle for Equal Schools: Mexican Americans during the Civil Rights Era* (Albany: State University of New York Press, 1997); Tyack and Hansot, *Learning Together*, ch. 9.

52. Zehm, "Misfits," appendix A.

53. Larry Cuban, "Yet to Be Taught: The Teacher and Student as Slow Learners," *Social Education* 34 (February 1970), 145–146; Kenneth B. Clark, *Dark Ghetto: Dilemmas of Social Power* (New York: Harper & Row, 1965).

54. James A. Banks and Cherry A. McGee Banks, eds., *Handbook of Research on Multicultural Education* (San Francisco: Jossey-Bass, 2001).

55. Executive Summary of the No Child Left Behind Act of 2001, Jan. 7, 2002, (PL107–110) at www. ed.gov/offices/oese/esea/summary.html

56. Thomas B. Fordham Foundation, *No Child Left Behind: What Will It Take?* (New York: Thomas B. Fordham Foundation, 2002).

57. William C. Symonds, "How to Fix America's Schools," *Business Week*, March 19, 2001, pp. 67, 67–80.

58. No Child Left Behind Act of 2001, p. 1.

59. Lauren B. Resnick, "The Mismeasure of Learning: Poorly Designed High-Stakes Tests May Undermine the Standards Movement" *Education Next* (Fall 2001): 78–83.

60. *New York Times,* Oct. 24, 2001, A20; Abigail Thernstrom, "Comments," in Fordham Foundation, *No Child,* pp. 103, 106.

5. Democracy in Education

1. Atwater quoted in Lewis C. Turner, "School-Board Minutes of One Hundred Years Ago," *The American School Board Journal* 100 (June 1940): 18, 91.

2. The pages of *The American School Board Journal* and political conflicts in local communities resonated with these issues. For a sample of the self-conceptions of the role of trustees see William George Bruce, "The Story of How We Got Our Start," *First in Education: The American School Board Journal—A Century of Service in School Leadership, 1891–1991,* supplement to *The American School Board Journal,* November 1991, p. A7 and passim; J. Leroy Thompson, "The Changing Concept of the Board of Education,"

The American School Board Journal 117 (October 1948): 20, 19–20; Martin E. Williams, "Qualities of a Good School Officer," *The American School Board Journal* 101 (August 1940): 25–26; J. R. Shannon, "What 1,000 Terre Haute Citizens Look for in Voting for School Board Members," *The American School Board Journal* 114 (February 1947): 29–30.

3. A fascinating cross-sectional view of U.S. education appears in James H. Blodgett, "Education," in *Report on Population of the United States at the Eleventh Census: 1890* (Washington, D.C.: Government Printing Office, 1897); his commentaries are as revealing as the statistics he compiles.

4. For praise of local control by Republican Senators John Ashcroft and Trent Lott, see Kathryn A. McDermott, *Controlling Public Education: Localism versus Equity* (Lawrence: University Press of Kansas, 1999), p. 13; Wallace D. Farnham, "The Weakened Spring of Government: A Study in Nineteenth Century American History," *American Historical Review* 68 (1963): 662–680; George F. Will, "Presidential Minimalism," *Newsweek*, March 20, 1995, p. 72; Stanley M. Elam, Lowell C. Rose, and Alex M. Gallup, "The 24th Annual Gallup / Phi Delta Kappa Poll of the Public's Attitudes toward the Public Schools," *Phi Delta Kappan* 74 (September 1992): 41–53.

5. William E. Chancellor, *Our Schools: Their Administration and Supervision* (Boston: D. C. Heath, 1915).

6. David Martin, "What Critics Won't See: If School Boards Vanished, We'd Have to Reinvent Them," *The American School Board Journal* 174 (April 1987): 29–30.

7. Charles H. Judd, "School Boards as an Obstruction to Good Administration," *The Nation's Schools* 13 (February 1934): 13–15; Judd, "The Place of the Board of Education," *Elementary School Journal* 33 (March 1933): 497–501; Myron Lieberman, *The Future of Public Education* (Chicago: University of Chicago Press, 1960), pp. 34–36; Rickover quoted in *First in Education*, p. A43; Chester E. Finn, "Reinventing Local Control," *Education Week*, January 23, 1991, pp. 40, 32; Dennis P. Doyle and Chester E. Finn, "American Schools and the Future of Local Control," *The Public Interest* 77 (Fall 1984): 77–95. School board advocates responded to Judd in M. R. Keyworth, "Why Boards of Education Are Both Desirable and Necessary," *The Nation's Schools* 13 (April 1934): 21–22.

8. Jacqueline P. Danzberger, "School Boards: Forgotten Players on the Education Team," *Phi Delta Kappan* 69 (September 1987): 53–59; Kennedy as quoted in Elaine Exton, "Will Local School Boards Flourish or Fade in the Great Society?" *The American School Board Journal* 150 (June 1965): 8, 7–8, 66–67.

9. David Tyack, Thomas James, and Aaron Benavot, *Law and the Shaping of Public Education, 1785–1954* (Madison: University of Wisconsin Press, 1987), epilogue; Susan H. Fuhrman and Richard F. Elmore, "Understanding Local Control in the Wake of State Education Reform," *Educational Evaluation and Policy Analysis* 12 (Spring 1990): 82–96; Fuhrman and Elmore note that the relations between states and local districts do not fit a zero-sum game in which states gain and localities lose "control"; the actual patterns of influence are more complicated. Sometimes reforms legislated by states reinforce what districts were already attempting to do; sometimes conflicting or unclear state regulations give leaders room to manoeuver; in the last decade or so, when many state departments of education have been losing staff, few state agencies have had enough time or expertise to enforce regulations.

10. Some exceptions to the scholarly neglect of districts are: Milbrey Wallin McLaughlin, "How District Communities Do and Do Not Foster Teacher Pride," *Educational Leadership* 50 (September 1992): 33–35; Stewart C. Purkey and Marshall S. Smith, "School Reform: The District Policy Implications of the Effective Schools Literature," *Elementary School Journal* 85, no. 2 (1985): 353–389; Richard F. Elmore, "The Role of Local School Districts in Instructional Improvement," in Susan H. Fuhrman, ed., *Designing Coherent Education Policy* (San Francisco: Jossey-Bass, 1993), pp. 96–124; Kathryn A. McDermott, *Controlling Public Education: Localism versus Equity* (Lawrence: University Press of Kansas, 1994).

11. The Jefferson quotation and Dewey's comment on him are in John Dewey, ed., *The Living Thoughts of Thomas Jefferson* (New York: Fawcett World Library, 1957), pp. 32, 30–32; Dewey's selection of Jefferson's writings and his commentaries on them create a kind of conversation between the two philosophers.

12. Wayne E. Fuller, *One-Room Schools of the Middle West* (Lawrence: University Press of Kansas, 1994), pp. 1, 4.

13. Farnham, "Weakened Spring"; Noel Sargent, "The California Constitutional Convention of 1878–79," *California Law Review* 6 (1917): 12; James Bryce, *The American Commonwealth* (New York: Macmillan and Co., 1888), vol. 2, pp. 238–241.

14. *The Marble Booster*, Jan. 29, 1916, in Oscar McCollum, Jr., *Marble: A Town Built on Dreams* (Silverton, Colo.: Sundance Publications, 1993), vol. 1, pp. 235–236.

15. Per Siljestrom, *The Educational Institutions of the United States: Their Character and Organization* (London: John Chapman, 1853), pp. 11, 39–42; David Tyack, "School Governance in the United States: Historical Puzzles

and Anomalies," in Jane Hannaway and Martin Carnoy, eds., *Decentralization and School Improvement: Can We Fulfill the Promise?* (San Francisco: Jossey-Bass Publishers, 1993), pp. 7–10.

16. Horace Mann, "Duties of School Committees," in *Educational Writings of Horace Mann* (Boston: Lee and Shepard, 1891), pp. 245–246.

17. Mann, "Duties," pp. 245–246; Theodore Lee Reller, *The Development of the City Superintendency of Schools in the United States* (Philadelphia: The Author, 1935); David B. Tyack, *The One Best System: A History of American Urban Education* (Cambridge: Harvard University Press, 1974), pp. 148–152.

18. Stanley K. Schultz, *The Culture Factory: Boston Public Schools, 1789–1860* (New York: Oxford University Press, 1973), pp. 34–39; Tyack, *One Best System,* pp. 154–156.

19. Adele Marie Shaw, "The Public Schools of a Boss-Ridden City," *World's Work,* 7 (October 1904): 5405–5414.

20. Ellwood P. Cubberley, *Rural Life and Education: A Study of the Rural-School Problem* (Boston: Houghton Mifflin, 1914); Cubberley, "Organization of Public Education," *NEA Addresses and Proceedings, 1915,* p. 95, pp. 91–97; Cubberley, *Public Education in the United States* (Boston: Houghton Miffli, 1919), pp. 316, 321, 719.

21. *First in Education,* p. A51; Williams, "Good School Officer," p. 25; Michael W. Kirst, "School Board: Evolution of an American Institution," in *First in Education,* pp. A13, A11–A14; Frank Slobetz, "The Village School-Board Member," *The American School Board Journal* 103 (July 1941): 16, 68.

22. Cubberley, *Rural-School Problem.*

23. Wayne E. Fuller, *The Old Country School: The Story of Rural Education in the Middle West* (Chicago: University of Chicago Press, 1982).

24. Perry G. Holden, "Our Rural Schools," *NEA Addresses and Proceedings, 1915,* p. 97, says that two thirds of students trained in rural schools; Newton Edwards and Herman G. Richey, *The School in the American Social Order: The Dynamics of American Education* (Boston: Houghton Mifflin, 1947), pp. 635, 688–699.

25. Andrew Gulliford, *America's Country Schools* (Washington, D.C.: Preservation Press, 1991), pp. 109, 108–111.

26. Ibid.; Fuller, *Old Country School.*

27. Joseph M. Cronin, *The Control of Urban Schools: Perspectives on the Power of Educational Reformers* (New York: The Free Press, 1973).

28. Ira Katznelson and Margaret Weir, *Schooling for All: Class, Race, and the Decline of the American Ideal* (New York: Basic Books, 1985); Raymond E. Callahan, *Education and the Cult of Efficiency: A Study of the Social Forces That*

Have Shaped the Administration of the Public Schools (Chicago: University of Chicago Press, 1962).

29. William T. Harris, "City School Supervision," *Educational Review* 3 (February 1892): 168–169; Chancellor, *Our Schools,* pp. 12–13; in the actual politics of progressive reform, as compared with the idealized blueprint of Cubberley, many grass-roots groups did participate: see William J. Reese, *Power and Promise of School Reform: Grassroots Movements during the Progressive Era* (Boston: Routledge and Kegan Paul, 1986).

30. C. G. Pearse, "Comment," *NEA Addresses and Proceedings, 1903,* p. 162; another superintendent ridiculed the notion that all school boards needed to do was to hand over the schools to the experts and then "take all the kicks and cuffs" that come from the community. "This is travesty," he said. "None of us believe such things, and we only talk this way when we are away from home. We are meek enough in the presence of our boards"— John W. Carr, "Comment," *NEA Addresses and Proceedings, 1903,* p. 159; for a critical study of the nonrepresentative character of school boards, see George S. Counts, *The Social Composition of Boards of Education* (Chicago: University of Chicago Press, 1927). On the left, scholars such as George Counts in the 1920s and Howard K. Beale in the 1930s said that school trustees took conservative positions on many issues ranging from unions to race because they represented elite interests and values. Counts wanted more representative democracy, not less—"Hell's Half Acre" needed representation, too.

31. Butler quoted in Chicago Merchants' Club, *Public Schools and Their Administration: Addresses Delivered at the Fifty-Ninth Meeting of the Merchants' Club of Chicago* (Chicago: Merchants' Club, 1906), p. 40; W. S. Ellis, "School Board Organization," *NEA Addresses and Proceedings, 1900,* pp. 633, 631–634; Lewis H. Jones, "The Best Methods of Electing School Boards," *NEA Addresses and Proceedings, 1903,* pp. 158–163; W. S. Deffenbaugh, "Practices and Concepts Relating to City Boards of Education," in U.S. Commissioner of Education, *Biennial Survey of Education in the United States, 1938–40* (Washington, D.C.: Government Printing Office, 1941), vol. 1, ch. 7.

32. Ellwood P. Cubberley, *Changing Conceptions of Education* (Boston: Houghton Mifflin, 1909), pp. 63, 56–57; David Alexander Gamson, "District by Design: Progressive Education Reform in Four Western Cities, 1900–1940" (Ph.D. diss., Stanford University, 2001); I am much indebted to conversations with David Gamson and to his thesis that deals with, among other topics, changing concepts of democracy among school leaders.

33. Julie A. Reuben, "Beyond Politics: Community Civics and the Redefinition of Citizenship in the Progressive Era," *History of Education Quarterly* 37 (Winter 1997): 399–420.

34. Ellwood P. Cubberley, *Public School Administration: A Statement of the Fundamental Principles Underlying the Organization and Administration of Public Education* (Boston: Houghton Mifflin, 1916); George D. Strayer, "Progress in City School Administration during the Past Twenty-Five Years," *School and Society* 32 (September 1930): 375–378; Theodore V. Quinlivan, "Changing Functions of Local School Boards," *The American School Board Journal* 98 (April 1939): 19–21; Lewis M. Terman, *Intelligence of School Children* (Boston: Houghton Mifflin, 1919), p. 73; Terman, ed., *Intelligence Tests and School Reorganization* (Yonkers-on-Hudson: World Book, 1922); Judith Rosenberg Raftery describes opposition to testing by teachers in *Land of Fair Promise: Politics and Reform in Los Angeles Schools, 1885–1941* (Stanford: Stanford University Press, 1992), ch. 5.

35. Jonathan Zimmerman, *Whose America? Culture Wars in the Public Schools* (Cambridge: Harvard University Press, 2002); Martin Luther King, *Why We Can't Wait* (New York: Harper & Row, 1964); David Kirp, *Just Schools: The Idea of Racial Equality in American Education* (Berkeley: University of California Press, 1982).

36. Vincent Harding, "The Black Wedge in America: Struggle, Crisis, and Hope, 1955–1975," *The Black Scholar* 7 (1975): 33; Robert Newby and David Tyack, "Victims without 'Crimes': Some Historical Perspectives on Black Education," *Journal of Negro Education* 40 (1971): 192–206.

37. Larry Cuban, *Urban School Chiefs under Fire* (Chicago: University of Chicago Press, 1976).

38. Ray Rist and Donald Anson, *Education, Social Science, and the Judicial Process* (New York: Teachers College Press, 1977); Kirp, *Just Schools;* Craig Peck, "'Educate to Liberate': The Black Panther Party and Political Education" (Ph.D.diss., Stanford University, 2002).

39. Henry Levin, "A Decade of Policy Developments in Improving Education and Training for Low-Income Populations," in Robert H. Havemann, ed., *A Decade of Federal Anti-Poverty Programs* (New York: Academic Press, 1977), pp. 123–188.

40. Anthony S. Bryk et al., *Charting Chicago School Reform: Democratic Localism as a Lever for Change* (Boulder: Westview Press, 1998); Henry Levin, ed., *Community Control of Schools* (Washington, D.C.: Brookings Institution, 1970); Michael B. Katz, "Chicago School Reform as History," *Teachers College Record* 94 (1992): 56–72.

41. David Tyack and Larry Cuban, *Tinkering toward Utopia: A Century of Public School Reform* (Cambridge: Harvard University Press, 1995), ch. 3.

42. John W. Meyer, *The Impact of the Centralization of Educational Funding and Control on State and Local Educational Governance* (Stanford: Institute for Research on Educational Finance and Governance, Stanford University, 1980).

43. William A. Firestone, Susan H. Fuhrman, and Michael W. Kirst, *The Progress of Reform: An Appraisal of State Education Initiatives* (New Brunswick, N.J.: Center for Policy Research in Education, 1989); David F. Labaree, *How to Succeed in School without Really Learning: The Credential Race in American Education* (New Haven: Yale University Press, 1997).

44. Labaree, *How to Succeed in School without Really Trying.*

45. Bryk et al., *Chicago School Reform;* Larry Cuban and Michael Usdan, *Powerful Reforms with Shallow Roots* (New York: Teachers College Press, 2002).

46. Robert J. Taggart, *Private Philanthropy and Public Education: Pierre S. DuPont and the Delaware Schools, 1890–1940* (Newark: University of Delaware Press, 1988).

47. Richard F. Elmore, "Testing Trap: The Single Largest—and Possibly Most Destructive—Federal Intrusion into America's Public Schools, *Harvard Magazine,* September-October, pp. 35, 35–37, 97; Romer quoted in Diana Jean Schemo, "Rule on Failing Schools Draws Criticism," *New York Times,* Nov. 28, 2002, p. A25.

48. Blodgett, "Education," p. 17.

49. Martin, "What Critics Won't See."

50. Jonathan Kozol, *Savage Inequalities: Children in America's Schools* (New York: Crown, 1991); McDermott, *Controlling Public Education.*

51. U.S. Department of Education, *Digest of Educational Statistics* (Washington, D.C.: Government Printing Office, 1997), table 90.

52. William W. Cutler III, *Parents and Schools: The 150-Year Struggle for Control in American Education* (Chicago: University of Chicago Press, 2000).

53. Mary Haywood Metz, "Real School: A Universal Drama amid Disparate Experience," in Douglas E. Mitchell and Margaret E. Goertz, eds., *Education Politics for the New Century* (New York: Falmer Press, 1990), pp. 75–91; Tyack and Cuban, *Tinkering,* ch. 4.

54. Martin, "What Critics Won't See," p. 29.

55. Garrett Ward Sheldon, *The Political Philosophy of Thomas Jefferson* (Baltimore: The Johns Hopkins University Press, 1991), pp. 60–62; David Mathews, *Is There a Public for Public Schools?* (Dayton, Ohio: Kettering Foundation Press, 1996).

6. Choices about Choice

1. Samuel G. Freedman, *Small Victories: The Real World of a Teacher, Her Students, and Their High School* (New York: Harper Perennial, 1990), pp. 100–101.

2. For a sampling of writings on choice, see *America 2000: An Education Strategy* (Washington, D.C.: U.S. Department of Education, 1990); *Voices from the Field: 30 Expert Opinions on America 2000, the Bush Administration Strategy to "Reinvent" America's Schools* (Washington, D.C.: William T. Grant Foundation, 1991); Isabel Wilkerson, "Private Schools Open Doors to Poor in Test," *New York Times,* Dec. 19, 1990, B9; John Leo, "School Reform's Best Choice," *U.S. News & World Report,* 110 (January 14, 1991): 17; "The Education President," *The New Republic* 198 (May 9, 1988): 5–7; Ben Wildavsky, "Hero of Choice," *The New Republic* 203 (October 22, 1990): 14–18; Joe Nathan, "The Rhetoric and the Reality of Expanding Educational Choices," *Phi Delta Kappan* 66 (March 1985): 476–481; Robert T. Carter, Faustine C. Jones-Wilson, and Nancy L. Arnez, "Demographic Characteristics of Greater Washington, D.C. Area Black Parents Who Chose Nonpublic Schooling for Their Young," *Journal of Negro Education* 58, no. 1(1989): 39–49; Lewis W. Finch, "Choice: Claims of Success, Predictions of Failure," *The Education Digest* 55 (November 1989): 12–15; Paul E. Peterson, "Choice in American Education," in Terry Moe, ed., *A Primer on America's Schools* (Stanford: Hoover Institution Press, 2001), pp. 249–284; Andrew J. Coulson, *Market Education: The Unknown History* (New Brunswick: Transaction Publishers, 1999); Amy Stuart Wells, *Time to Choose: America at the Crossroads of School Choice Policy* (New York: Hill and Wang, 1993).

3. Mario D. Fantini, "Options for Students, Parents, and Teachers: Public Schools of Choice," *Phi Delta Kappan* 52 (May 1971): 541–43; Peter W. Cookson, Jr., *School Choice: The Struggle for the Soul of American Education* (New Haven: Yale University Press, 1994); Rob Reich, *Bridging Liberalism and Multiculturalism in American Education* (Chicago: University of Chicago Press, 2002), ch. 6.

4. For a variety of studies of choice plans within public education see William H. Clune and John F. Witte, eds., *Choice and Control in American Education: The Practice of Choice, Decentralization, and School Restructuring* (New York: The Falmer Press, 1990), vol. 2, pp. 1–222; John F. Witte, *Choice in American Education* (Madison, Wisc.: Robert M. LaFollette Institute of Public Affairs, 1990); Association for Supervision and Curriculum Development, *Public Schools of Choice* (Alexandria, Va.: ASCD, 1990).

5. Milton and Rose Friedman, *Free to Choose: A Personal Statement* (New York: Harcourt Brace Johanovich, 1979), ch. 6; John E. Chubb and Terry,

M. Moe, *Politics, Markets, and America's Schools* (Washington, D.C.: The Brookings Institution, 1990); Myron Lieberman, *Privatization and Educational Choice* (New York: St. Martin's Press, 1989).

6. James R. Rinehart and Jackson F. Lee, Jr., *Public Education and the Dynamics of Choice* (New York: Praeger, 1991); for an argument for choice that relies more on the child's interest and the rights of families than on claims about the market, see John E. Coons and Stephen D. Sugarman, *Education by Choice: The Case for Family Control* (Berkeley: University of California Press, 1978).

7. John F. Witte, "Choice and Control: An Analytic Overview," in Clune and Witte, eds., *Choice and Control*, vol. 1, pp. 22, 13, 11–46; Robert B. Everhart, ed., *The Public School Monopoly: A Critical Analysis of Education and the State in American Society* (Cambridge: Ballinger Publishing Co., 1982).

8. Richard Rubinson, "Class Formation, Politics, and Institutions: Schooling in the United States," *American Journal of Sociology* 92 (November 1986): 519–543; Arthur G. Powell, Eleanor Farrar, and David K. Cohen, *The Shopping Mall High School: Winners and Losers in the Educational Marketplace* (Boston: Houghton Mifflin, 1985).

9. Larry Cuban and Dorothy Shipps, eds., *Reconstructing the Common Good in Education: Coping with Intractable American Dilemmas* (Stanford: Stanford University Press, 2000); Henry Levin, "The Theory of Choice Applied to Education," in Clune and Witte, eds., *Choice and Control*, vol. 1, pp. 247–284; Abigail Thernstrom, "Is Choice a Necessity?" *The Public Interest* 101 (Fall 1990): 124–132; Nicholas Lemann, "A False Panacea," *The Atlantic Monthly* 267 (January 1991): 101–105; David Kirp, "School Choice Is a Panacea, These Authors Say," *The American School Board Journal* 177 (September 1990): 38, 41; Robert Lowe, "Neither Excellence Nor Equity for All: The Perilous Consequences of Choice," *Rethinking Schools* (January-February 1991): 3–4; Susan Anderson, "Drawn off Course: Like a Seductive Siren Song the Market Rhetoric of School Choice Lures Us Away from Facing our True Educational Crisis," *California Tomorrow* 4 (Fall 1989): 6–13.

10. Carl F. Kaestle, *Pillars of the Republic: Common Schools and American Society, 1780–1860* (New York: Hill and Wang, 1983), ch. 3; E. G. West, "The Political Economy of American Public School Legislation," *Journal of Law and Economics* 10 (October 1967): 101–128.

11. Theodore R. Sizer, ed., *The Age of the Academies* (New York: Teachers College Press, 1964); Michael B. Katz, *Reconstructing American Education* (Cambridge: Harvard University Press, 1987), ch. 2.

12. James H. Blodgett, "Education," in *Report on Population of the United States at the Eleventh Census: 1890* (Washington , D.C.: Government Printing Of-

fice, 1987), p. 17, pp. 1–116; William T. Harris and Duane Doty, educational leaders, wrote a statement of public school principles agreed to by many of their colleagues, suggesting a growing consensus—*A Statement of the Theory of Education in the United States as Approved by Many Leading Educators* (Washington, D.C.: Government Printing Office, 1874; on the general distrust of government, see David Tyack, Thomas James, and Aaron Benavot, *Law and the Shaping of Public Education, 1785–1954* (Madison: University of Wisconsin Press, 1987), pt. 2.

13. Wayne E. Fuller, *The Old Country School: The Story of Rural Education in the Middle West* (Chicago: University of Chicago Press, 1982).

14. Blodgett, "Education," p. 21; Robert H. Wiebe, *Self Rule: A Cultural History of American Democracy* (Chicago: University of Chicago Press, 1995).

15. Thomas James, "Questions about Educational Choice: An Argument from History," in Thomas James and Henry M. Levin, eds., *Public Dollars for Private Schools: The Case of Tuition Tax Credits* (Philadelphia: Temple University Press, 1983), p. 64.

16. Statistics on nonpublic schools are approximate at best. A good source for the late nineteenth century is the census monograph on education by James H. Blodgett, *Report on Population of the United States at the Eleventh Census: 1890*, pt. II, pp. 1–116. On the basis of reports from schools, Blodgett finds that about 8 percent of pupils in elementary and secondary schools were enrolled in denominational/parochial schools (65 percent of them in Catholic schools); in descending order of magnitude of students, the religious groups were Catholic, Lutheran, Methodist, Presbyterian, Baptist, and Congregational. Blodgett notes, however, that it is hard to tell from school reports if these religious schools were purely "private" or "public." In the twentieth century, according to Otto F. Kraushaar, the percent of students in private schools fluctuated over time: 1900, 7.6; 1910 8.6; 1920, 7.3; 1930, 9.4; 1940, 9.3; 1950, 11.9; 1960, 13.6; 1970, 11—*American Nonpublic Schools: Patterns of Diversity* (Baltimore: The Johns Hopkins University Press, 1972), p. 14, table 1, pp. 5–6. Two useful surveys of nonpublic schools in 1960–61 by Diane B. Gertler showed that 94 percent of private elementary schools and 60 percent of secondary schools were church-related—*Statistics of Nonpublic Elementary Schools, 1960–6*, and *Statistics of Nonpublic Secondary Schools, 1960–61* (Washington, D.C.: Government Printing Office, 1961). Also see James C. Carper and Thomas C. Hunt, *Religious Schooling in America* (Birmingham, Ala.: Religious Education Press, 1984), pp. ix, 1.

17. James W. Fraser, *Between Church and State: Religion and Public Education in a Multicultural America* (New York: St. Martin's Press, 1999).

18. The Catholic is quoted in Robert D. Cross, "Origins of the Catholic Parochial School in America," *The American Benedictine Review* 16 (June 1965): 197, 194–209; for a perceptive critique of the current discourse on choice, see Eric Bredo, "Choice, Constraint, and Community," in William Lowe Boyd and Charles Taylor Kerchner, eds., *The Politics of Excellence and Choice in Education* (New York: The Falmer Press, 1987).

19. Horace Bushnell, "Christianity and Common Schools," *Common School Journal* 2 (February 15, 1940): 58; Lloyd P. Jorgenson, *The State and the Non-Public School, 1825–1925* (Columbia: University of Missouri Press, 1987), chs. 2–4.

20. Winthrop Hudson, *American Protestantism* (Chicago: University of Chicago Press, 1961), ch. 2; David Tyack, "The Kingdom of God and the Common School: Protestant Ministers and the Educational Awakening in the West," *Harvard Educational Review*, 36 (Fall 1966): 447–469.

21. As quoted in Thomas James, "Rights of Conscience and State School Systems in Nineteenth-Century America," in Paul Finkelman and Stephen E. Gottlieb, eds., *Toward a Usable Past: Liberty under State Constitutions* (Athens, Ga.: University of Georgia Press, 1991), pp. 128, 117–147.

22. Donohue v. Richards, 38 Me. 376 (1854); William Kailer Dunn, *What Happened to Religious Education? The Decline of Religious Teaching in the Public Elementary School, 1776–1861* (Baltimore: The Johns Hopkins University Press, 1958), pp. 373–375; Benjamin Justice, "Peaceable Adjustments: Religious Diversity and Local Control in New York State Public Schools, 1865–1900" (Ph.D. diss., Stanford University, 2002).

23. Donohue v. Richards, 38 Me. 376, 410 (1854); Fraser, *Church and State;* Irish Catholics of Boston were common targets of the Boston School Board, which said that Irish newcomers needed the strongest doses of "moral and religious teaching, powerful enough if possible to keep them in the right path amid the moral darkness which is their daily and domestic walk . . . unless we can redeem this population in their childhood by moral means, we must control them by force, or support them as paupers, at a maturer period of life." Not surprisingly, textbooks used in many cities vilified the Roman Church and denigrated the new immigrants. Boston board quoted in Charles Leslie Glenn, *The Myth of the Common School* (Amherst: The University of Massachusetts Press, 1988), p. 202.

24. For analysis of the different world-views of these groups, see Glenn, *Myth,* and Jorgenson, *Non-Public School,* chs. 5–6; for studies of religious conflict in cities, see Diane Ravitch, *The Great School Wars: New York City, 1805–1973* (New York: Basic Books, 1976); James W. Sanders, *The Edu-*

cation of an Urban Minority: Catholics in Chicago, 1833–1965 (New York: Oxford University Press, 1977); F. Michael Perko, *A Time to Favor Zion: The Ecology of Religion and School Development on the Urban Frontier, Cincinnati, 1830–1870* (Chicago: Educational Studies Press, 1988).

25. Cross, "Origins of the Catholic Parochial School, in America," pp. 201–202, 194–209; Neil G. McCluskey, S.J., *Catholic Education Faces Its Future* (Garden City, N.Y.: Doubleday, 1969), pp. 82–83; Kraushaar, *Nonpublic Schools,* p. 24.

26. Ward M. McAfee, *Religion, Race, and Reconstruction: The Public School in the Politics of the 1870s* (Albany: State University of New York Press, 1998); Thomas Nast, "The American River Ganges," *Harper's Weekly,* September 1871; Jorgenson, *Non-Public Schools,* ch. 6; David Tyack, "Onward Christian Soldiers: Religion in the American Common School, 1870–1900," in Paul Nash, ed., *History and Education* (New York: Random House, 1970), pp. 212–255; Protestant denominations that ran their own religious schools—such as the Lutherans—might also have benefited from public subsidies, but one reason they did not press hard for government funding seems to have been a fear that Catholics would also receive government support for their parochial schools—see August C. Stellhorn, *Schools of the Lutheran Church–Missouri Synod* (St. Louis: Concordia Publishing House, 1963), p. 239, passim, and Walter H. Beck, *Lutheran Elementary Schools in the United States: A History of the Development of Parochial Schools and Synodical Educational Policies and Programs* (St. Louis: Concordia Publishing House, 1939); on the anti-Catholicism of liberal intellectuals, see John T. McGreevy, "Thinking on One's Own: Catholicism in the American Intellectual Imagination, 1928–1960," *Journal of American History* 84 (June 1997): 97–131.

27. I am indebted to William Tobin for pointing out the language of duty and collective action in the writings of leaders in religious schooling; Carper and Hunt, *Religious Schooling.*

28. Stellhorn, *Schools of the Lutheran Church,* pp. 66, 58, 89, 239, passim; Beck, *Lutheran Elementary Schools;* Victor C. Krause, ed., *Lutheran Elementary Schools in Action* (St. Louis: Concordia Publishing Co., .d.); Kraushaar, *Nonpublic Schools,* pp. 34, 33–35; Joseph Kaminetsky, "The Jewish Day Schools—Rapidly Growing Movement," *Phi Delta Kappan* 45 (December 1963): 141–44; Clemmont E. Vontress, "The Black Muslim Schools—Threat, Blessing, or Both?" *Phi Delta Kappan* 47 (October 1965): 86–90; Jon Diefenthaler, "Lutheran Schools in America," in Carper and Hunt, *Religious Schooling,* pp. 35–57; George R. Knight, "Seventh-Day Adventist Education: A Historical Sketch and Profile," ibid., pp. 85–109; Eduardo

Rauch, "The Jewish Day School in America: A Critical History and Contemporary Dilemmas," ibid., pp. 130–168; James C. Carver, "The Christian Day School," ibid., pp. 110–129.

29. David Tyack and Thomas James, "Moral Majorities and the School Curriculum: Historical Perspectives on the Legalization of Virtue," *Teachers College Record*, 86, no. 4 (1985): 513–537; on Oregon see Pierce v. Society of Sisters, 268 U.S. 510 (1925); Jorgenson, *Non-Public School*, chs. 9–10; David Tyack, "The Perils of Pluralism: The Background of the Pierce Case," *American Historical Review*, 74 (October 1968): 74–98.

30. Fraser, *Between Church and State*, chs. 7–10; Carver, "Christian Day School," pp. 115–117.

31. Powell, Farrar, and Cohen, *Shopping Mall.*

32. National Commission on Excellence in Education, *A Nation at Risk* (Washington, D.C.: Government Printing Office, 1983), pp. 2–4; Policy Information Center, *What Americans Study* (Princeton: Educational Testing Service, 1989), pp. 2–6.

33. Edward A. Krug, *The Shaping of the American High School, 1920–1941* (Madison: University of Wisconsin Press, 1972); Powell, Farrar, and Cohen, *Shopping Mall*, ch. 5; Robert Hampel, *The Last Little Citadel: American High Schools since 1940* (Boston: Houghton Mifflin, 1986); Edward L. Thorndike, "A Neglected Aspect of the American High School," *Educational Review* 33 (1907): 254; the larger size of high schools permitted differentiation by sex and class—see Millicent Rutherford, "Feminism and the Secondary School Curriculum, 1890–1920" (Ph.D. diss., Stanford University, 1977).

34. Logan C. Osterndorf and Paul J. Horn, *Course Offerings, Enrollments, and Curriculum Practices in Public Secondary Schools, 1972–73* (Washington, D.C.: Government Printing Office, 1976), pp. 5, 6, 13, 11, 4–21; Grace S. Wright, *Subject Offerings and Enrollments in Public Secondary Schools* (Washington, D.C.: Government Printing Office, 1965), p. 19, 1–18; Powell, Farrar, and Cohen, *Shopping Mall*, p. 11; David L. Angus and Jeffrey E. Mirel, *The Failed Promise of the American High School* (New York: Teachers College Press, 1999); Diane Ravitch, *Left Back: A Century of Failed School Reforms* (New York: Simon Schuster, 2000).

35. Osterndorf and Horn, *Offerings*, p. 11.

36. Center for Education Statistics, *The Condition of Education, 1987* (Washington, D.C.: Government Printing Office, 1987), pp. 84–87; for statistics on changes in course-taking patterns in the late 1980s, see Policy Information Center, *What Americans Study.*

37. Powell, Farrar, and Cohen, *Shopping Mall*, p. 259.

38. Ibid.; Richard F. Elmore, "Choice in Public Education," Center for Policy Research in Education, JNE-01, December 1986, p. 33; Theodore Sizer, *Horace's Compromise: The Dilemma of the American High School* (Boston: Houghton Mifflin, 1984); Ernest Boyer, *High School: A Report on Secondary Education in America* (New York: Harper, 1985).

39. Theodore Sizer, "Foreword," in Hampel, *Citadel,* p. xi.

40. Powell, Farrar, and Cohen, *Shopping Mall,* p. 259; David Tyack and Elisabeth Hansot, *Learning Together: A History of Coeducation in American Public Schools* (Cambridge: Harvard University Press, 1990), chs. 7–8; Hampel, *Citadel,* pp. 10–11; Jeannie Oakes, *Keeping Track* (New Haven: Yale University Press, 1985).

41. Elmore, "Choice in Public Education," pp. 33–34; Powell, Farrar, and Cohen, *Shopping Mall,* p. 259; Sizer, *Horace's Compromise;* Boyer, *High School.*

42. Jeffrey Henig, *Rethinking School Choice: Limits of the Market Metaphor* (Princeton: Princeton University Press, 1994); Bruce Fuller and Richard F. Elmore, with Gary Orfield, *Who Chooses? Who Loses? Culture, Institutions, and the Unequal Effects of School Choice* (New York: Teachers College Press, 1996.

43. Gary A. Orfield, "Do We Know Anything Worth Knowing about Educational Effects of Magnet Schools?" in Clune and Witte, eds., *Choice and Control,* vol. 2, pp. 119–123; Donald R. Moore and Suzanne Davenport, "School Choice: The New Improved Sorting Machine," in William Lowe Boyd and Herbert J. Walberg, eds., *Choice in Education: Potential and Problems* (Berkeley: McCutchan Publishing Corp., 1990), ch. 9; Orfield, "Magnet Schools," pp. 119–124.

44. Bruce Fuller, ed., *Inside Charter Schools: The Paradox of Radical Decentralization* (Cambridge: Harvard University Press, 2000), ch. 2; Peter S. Lewis, "Private Education and the Subcultures of Dissent: Alternative/Free Schools (1965–1975) and Christian Fundamentalist Schools (1965–1990) (Ph.D. diss., Stanford University, 1991). Dan A. Lewis compares the deregulation and privatization of mental health care and of education—did these help those most in need? See Dan A. Lewis, "Deinstitutionalization and School Decentralization: Making the Same Mistake Twice," in Jane Hannaway and Martin Carnoy, eds., *Decentralization and School Improvement: Can We Fulfill the Promise?* (San Francisco: Jossey-Bass, 1993), pp. 84–101.

45. Seymour Fliegel, "Creative Non-Compliance," in Clune and Witte, eds., *Choice and Control,* vol. 2, p. 201.

46. Fliegel, "Non-Compliance," pp. 199–222.

47. Fliegel, "Non-Compliance," pp. 207, 199–222; Deborah W. Meier, "Choice Can Save Public Education," *The Nation* 252 (March 4, 1991): 270, 253, 266–71; Meier, *The Power of Their Ideas: Lessons for America from a Small School in Harlem* (Boston: Beacon Press, 1995).

48. Richard F. Elmore, "Would Choice + Competition Yield Quality Education?" and Gary Orfield, "Choice, Testing, and the Reelection of a President," in *Voices from the Field,* pp. 3–4, 7–8; John Chubb and Terry Moe, "America's Public Schools: Choice IS a Panacea," *The Brookings Review* (Summer 1990): 233–267.

Acknowledgments

I am deeply grateful to the Spencer Foundation for supporting this research and writing and to the Stanford Humanities Center for a stimulating sabbatical year when I began work on this book.

I appreciate the opportunity to take part in four workshops dealing with issues that are central in this book. The first analyzed cultural conflict and common ground in American society and took place at the Center for Advanced Study in the Behavioral Sciences at Stanford. The second, held in Santa Fe under the auspices of the Social Science Research Council, dealt with the political incorporation of immigrants. The third, at Stanford, dealt with reconstructing the common good in education. And the fourth, focusing on democracy in education, was at the School of Education of the University of Pennsylvania.

I'm indebted to friends and colleagues for thoughtful conversations and critiques that blended timely encouragement and astute suggestions for revision. Some have read the whole manuscript and helped me recast the argument: Mark Brilliant, Eammon Callan, Larry Cuban, Patricia Albjerg Graham, Elisabeth Hansot, Benjamin Justice, Michael Katz, Rob Kunzman, Susan Lloyd, Ray McDermott, Rob Reich, John Rury, Ingrid Seyer, Dorothy Shipps, Julie Williams, Joy Williamson, and Jonathan Zimmerman. Others have commented on portions of the book in its several previous incarnations and suggested useful alternative interpretations: Sarah Deschenes, Ruben Donato, Paula Fass, David Gamson, Gary Gerstle, Harvey Kantor, David Labaree, Ellen Lagemann, Marvin Lazerson, Bob Lowe, John Meyer, Ted Mitchell, Craig Peck, Daniel Perlstein, William Reese, Neil Smelser, Sandy Stein, Guadalupe Valdes, and Diane Wood. My thanks to all of them for their good advice and warm support.

This is the fifth book on which editor Nancy Clemente and I have collaborated since 1967, to my great good fortune. I thank Nancy for her candor and wit, her skill and good sense, and her blending of the virtues of Indiana and New England.

I appreciate permission to adapt for this book some essays originally written as articles in journals or as chapters in books:

"Preserving the Republic by Educating Republicans," in Neil J. Smelser and Jeffrey C. Alexander, eds., *Diversity and Its Discontents: Cultural Conflict and Common Ground in Contemporary American Society* (Princeton: Princeton University Press, 1999), pp. 63–83.

"School for Citizens: The Politics of Civic Education from 1790 to 1990, "in Gary Gerstle and John Mollenkopf, eds., *E Pluribus Unum? Contemporary and Historian Perspectives on Immigrant Political Incorporation* (New York: Russell Sage Foundation, 2001), pp. 331–370; ©2001 Russell Sage Foundation, 112 East 64th Street, New York, NY 10021.

"Monuments between Covers: The Politics of Textbooks," *American Behavioral Scientist* 42 (March 1999): 992–931; ©1999 Sage Publications, Inc.

"Constructing Difference: Historical Reflections on Schooling and Social Diversity," *Teachers College Record* 95 (Fall 1993): 1–34.

With Sarah Deschenes and Larry Cuban, "Mismatch: Historical Perspectives on Schools and Students Who Don't Fit Them," *Teachers College Record* 103 (August 1999): 525–547.

Index